THE FOUR HORSEMEN
The Flames of War in the Third World

THE FOUR

With photographs by the author

HORSEMEN

The Flames of War in the Third World

by David Munro

Lyle Stuart   *Secaucus, New Jersey*

Published by Lyle Stuart Inc.
120 Enterprise Ave., Secaucus, N.J. 07094
In Canada: Musson Book Company
a division of General Publishing Co. Limited
Don Mills, Ontario

Manufactured in the United States of America

Library of Congress Cataloging-in-Publication Data

Munro, David.
   The four horsemen.

   Bibliography: p.
   1. Developing countries—Military relations—United
States.   2. United States—Military relations—
Developing countries.   3. Developing countries—History,
Military.   I. Title.   II. Title: 4 horsemen.
D888.U6M86   1987   355′.0332′1724   87-6496
ISBN 0-8184-0441-8

For
TRUAN and all the children

Acknowledgments

Without the help of the following people in making the three documentary films on which this book is based, the book itself might not have been possible.

I would like to thank: Ivan Strasburg for his very special way of seeing, his friendship, laughter and trust, all of which he gave me through many bizarre, sometimes frightening, situations, and Eddie Tise for his gentleness, enthusiasm, his innocence, and fresh ideas, and both of them for their wonderful conversations. Gerry Pinches for sticking by me when the going got rough. Cherry Farrow who gave up a trip to China to work with me and put up with my single-mindedness and impulsiveness and who was always there for over three sometimes difficult years throughout which she managed against great odds to talk some sense into me. Mike Rossiter to whom I was a "looney" and still his loyalty was unshakable, his incredibly incisive mind a joy and his courage an example.

Thanks too to: Biddy Richards, John Richardson, Mike Scott, Ahmed, Toobe & The Captain, Gebrehuit, Te'ame Tewolde Berhan, Samson Mahari and Cham Borey, all of whom gave of their knowledge and unselfishly of their time. Julia Kennedy, June Peacock and Janice Hartree, to whom I was mostly an infuriating voice on the other end of a phone far away, asking the impossible and invariably getting it. Noel Smart, Mel Marr, Mike McDuffy, Eoin McCann, Steve Phillips, Peter Smith and Colin Martin for coming part of the way with me and Keith Byres who was there at the end with wonderful bacon sarnies and cans of cool beer; John Hall who appeared late with a refreshing appreciation of film.

My thanks to Richard Creasey of Central Independent Television who had the courage to back me and the patience to wait till I was done.

Special thanks and appreciation are due to MacBrown who was the greatest nanny my baby could have had. His stamina and dedication, his selflessness and expertise contributed in no small part to the best unfolding of the story.

Special thanks are also due to Gordon Limb who gave so much to this book and out of friendship and kindness worked unending hours with me printing the stills.

To my family and close friends for their unfailing encouragement and understanding, and to my father, the kindest man I have ever known, for never trying to suppress the wanderer in me and for teaching me to question everything.

Finally Bobby Muller, who was the first person to listen to my early, rambling thoughts for the book and the films. Having listened he said, "You know, I know that everything you're telling me is true but that's the craziest idea I've heard in a long time," then after a pause he added, "It's so crazy I think you should do it." Thank you, Bobby.

Contents

AND FROM THE BROKEN SEAL
LEAPED A FLAME COLOURED STEED.
HIS RIDER BRANDISHED OVER HIS HEAD
AN ENORMOUS SWORD.
HE WAS WAR.
PEACE FLED FROM THE WORLD
BEFORE HIS FURIOUS GALLOP;
HUMANITY WAS GOING TO BE EXTERMINATED.

—BLASCO-IBANEZ, *The Four Horsemen of the Apocalypse*

Introduction

This is not simply a photographic book. It is not intended to end up as a "coffee table decoration."

It is a collection of moments and stories—in pictures, the words of ordinary people, and interviews—that I witnessed in the fifteen months between January 1984 and March 1985.

I began with the almost abstract, I suppose academic, idea of wanting to show the extent to which the world is at war, the rampant unnecessary suffering, the despair and waste of it all. I also wanted to try to provide a succinct background to these conflicts: some of the less obvious reasons and stories that lie beneath them which are so often ignored by the media, leaving us at a loss to understand them. Finally, I wanted to attempt to explain how the developed nations, East and West, have convinced themselves that they need these wars as export markets for weaponry.

All those intentions remain and are present here, but as I travelled from one war zone to another—some that I already knew, others that I was witnessing for the first time—my abstract idea had a head-on collision with reality. For although I wasn't exactly a newcomer to some of these conflicts, by experiencing them collectively rather than individually, as is the rule, I was stunned by the enormity, the extent of the madness.

The gulf between academic knowledge and the reality of first-hand experience is too great; neither imagination nor any amount of cold sanitized information can bridge it—only images, sounds and smells can do that. I hope, therefore, that what follows conveys, if nothing else, the breadth of this worsening dilemma that currently threatens our world.

What I came to understand in those fifteen months was the truly universal extent of war today. The stories of barbarism and despair are universal, and concern or help by the provision of aid, from West or East, are conditioned not by human suffering and need but by "political considerations." I also came to see, with a fresh and I suppose privileged insight, what "political considerations" really means.

It does not mean consideration for ideological or politically partisan belief, as one might assume, but the strategic, which in turn means economic, designs that the developed world has upon the third world and over which they battle.

Introduction

It appears that historians have varying views as to when the seeds of this struggle were sown. Some say the eighteenth century, others place it in the nineteenth around the time of President Monroe when the United States assumed the right of dominance over all of the Americas before, by the 1920s, turning its attention to Europe. But Tsarist Russia and latterly the Soviet Union soon recognized that she was to be the other player.

By the end of World War II the pubescent super powers had consolidated their control over their regions and the majority of those nations in the north that they desired as allies or markets, and as the European empires receded they began to turn their attention to the dominions of those empires. Together with their allies in Europe, both the United States and the Soviet Union have, for the past forty years, preached the ideology of the Cold War, creating the belief that the two camps have been locked in a desperate struggle for national survival and for the hearts and minds of the rest of the world, almost as if they have been waging an altruistic crusade to save the poorer nations from the damnation of the other's influence. In truth, concern for the hearts and minds and therefore well-being of the Third World has always been very low on the list of priorities.

The super powers have utilized the opportunities created by struggles for independence from colonial domination, traditional animosities or tribal and territorial disputes. They have watched these confrontations smouldering and then fanned the flames of war with conditional aid and, increasingly, modern weaponry which the smaller nations are made to believe they need if they are to enter the twentieth century and the developed world.

So the conflict is not in truth ideological, but rather the case of the developed nations of the north using the peoples of the lesser developed nations as proxies who fight and die in order that they win, not independence for themselves, but the right for West or East to exploit these nations either economically, strategically, or both. I do not believe that this is a grand conspiracy, though the carving up of Europe at the end of the Second World War was a pragmatic compromise acceptable to both sides, and certain evidence from the United States suggests that the policy, conspiracy or not, has been well defined for some considerable time. Furthermore, it would be foolish to suggest that the super powers have created all the wars that have raged since the end of World War II, though the list of those that they have started is an indictment in itself. Rather, I believe it is a habit and, possibly, the immoral, ignorant and unacceptable progression from the policy of direct colonial rule.

The paradox, however, and the proof that the North is not quite as clever as it believes it is, is that this process is destroying the very wealth that the developed world so avariciously desires by devastating societies that are ill-equipped in the first place to cope with the physical and social destruction caused by modern warfare, and thereby halting economic and social development within those societies which would be of benefit to everyone. Meanwhile it is seriously threatening the economic and actual survival of all parties.

I am not a pacifist but I could never support or justify casting the first blow. Adequate armaments and men to ensure the defense of national borders are still a necessity, for I do not believe that the human race has yet acquired sufficient collective wisdom to totally disarm; one can only speculate in which millennium that Utopian development might occur. But there is a great difference between offense and defense; too often stronger groups and nations opt for the former in the name of the latter and I believe it is therefore right for people who are being attacked to defend themselves. But, war is a stupid way of doing business, for that in the end is what it's all about, and unless we find another way, a peaceful way, soon there will be no wars to fight because there will be no countries, no resources and no people left to fight over.

Each one of these so-called "little wars" leads the world closer to the possibility of a real super-power confrontation and "the war to end all wars" and all of us—an Intercontinental Nuclear War.

As my fifteen-month journey progressed I stopped seeing facial or cultural characteristics. What I saw and heard instead, in many tongues, was the same fear, the same sound, the same stories of brutality, the same anger, hatred and feelings of total helplessness. I also came across some of the bravest people it is possible to meet. Men, women and children who, despite the havoc, carnage and selfishness around them, are able to carry on, to smile and attempt some semblance of normality, humanity and generosity in their fractured lives.

It is to them that this book is dedicated.

PART ONE

"You cannot call this peace"

"You cannot call this peace"

During the 1982 election campaign in Britain, Margaret Thatcher stated that nuclear weapons "had helped to keep the peace for nearly forty years."[1]

> "That's what they mean by peace, they mean we haven't had a nuclear war, but every other kind of war has been taking place and if you call that peace then it is really a profound denial of what's going on. The casualty figures since the end of World War Two for all the wars fought come to about 30 million people, which exceeds the number of Soviet dead, both military and civilian, in World War Two, and eventually we will exceed the number of all dead in World War Two. So it seems to me that this is a complete lie. You cannot call this peace."—TOM GERVASI, Director, Center for Military Research

Since the end of World War Two there have been well over 100 major wars. The academics seem unable to agree upon an exact figure, largely because they all appear to use different criteria to determine when a war *is* a war. However, they all seem to arrive at a figure somewhere between 100 and 150. Similarly and for the same reasons, there seems to be little agreement on the number of interventions in these conflicts by the super powers. Using the criterion of actual military involvement, I calculate that the Soviet Union and its allies have intervened militarily in 18 foreign wars whereas the United States and its allies have been involved in 33, and it is almost impossible to find a war where one or both of them have not been indirectly involved. This imbalance, roughly two Western interventions to one Eastern, may be a bitter pill for Western Cold Warriors to swallow and may also permit propagandists in the Kremlin to point accusatory fingers westward, but all the academics appear to agree on the ratio and therefore it is only the degree of their guilt that differs, which in the end is irrelevant.

In the fifties there were, on average, nine countries at war every year. By the seventies that average had risen to fourteen and the rise continued—by 1984 it had reached eighteen.

Today, if you board a plane at London's Heathrow Airport and fly for just three hours—one if you care to go to Ulster—you will hit a war. Thereafter, a flight of just two hours, in almost any direction, will land you in another—and you can keep on going, right around the planet.

World War III is not the fabled apocalypse of the future, it is happening now.

> "If you look back over the course of American foreign policy toward the Third World and toward the Soviet Union since World War Two, it has this fundamental continuity of trying to transfer the hostilities toward Communism into the struggle for resources and markets in the Third World.... Because of the nuclear stalemate it's too dangerous to have a real conflict in the First World, so all the fighting and dying takes place in the

Third World. Yet the tensions are really in the First World....It's one of the ways in which the Third World, in this post-colonial period, is still being exploited in a very fundamental way. That's not to deny that the very deep changes that are brought about by the decolonization process wouldn't have generated a lot of conflicts in any event, but those conflicts I think have been deepened and expanded and carried on with much more modern weaponry as a result of the rivalry between the super-powers and their allies that has been exported to the Third World. We speak of maintaining peace but it's maintaining peace at the center, at the expense of those at the periphery of world power."—RICHARD A. FALK, Milbank Professor of International Law and Practice, Princeton University

In 1948, George Kennan, who was Head of Policy Planning at the U.S. Department of State, stated in a top secret internal foreign policy memorandum:

"...we have about 50 percent of the world's wealth but only 6.3 percent of it's population....*Our real task in the coming period is to devise a pattern of relationships which will permit us to maintain this position of disparity without positive detriment to our national security.* To do so, we will have to dispense with all sentimentality and day-dreaming; and our attention will have to be concentrated everywhere on our immediate national objectives. *We need not deceive ourselves that we can afford the luxury of altruism and world benefaction....*

"The peoples of Asia and of the Pacific are going to go ahead, whatever we do, with the development of their political forms and mutual interrelationships in their own way.... This process of adaptation will also be long and violent. It is not only possible, but probable, that in the course of this process many peoples will fall, for varying periods, under the influence of Moscow, whose ideology has a greater lure for such peoples, and probably greater reality, than anything we could oppose to it....In the face of this situation we would be better off to dispense now with a number of the concepts which have underlined our thinking....*We should cease to talk about vague and unreal objectives such as human rights, the raising of living standards, and democratization.* The day is not far off when we are going to have to deal in straight power concepts. The less we are hampered by idealistic slogans, the better."[2] [Emphasis added]

"This is what was being said behind closed doors of the State Department some 30 years ago and led us into Vietnam, to 'protect our interests.' It's the same self-interest we're protecting in the guise of national security and the guise of democracy that's leading us into Central America...."
—DR. CHARLIE CLEMMENTS, M.D.

NICARAGUA

"Sooner or later, every nation, however weak, achieves freedom"

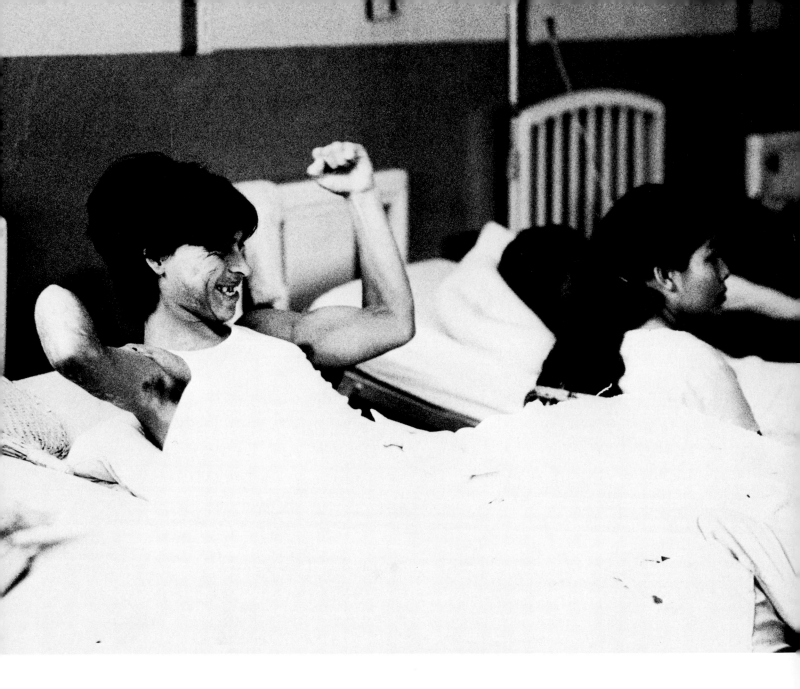

"*Who do you blame?*"

"The Contras of course, and the North Americans."

"*Why?*"

"Because I was too young to participate in the Triumph [the overthrow of Somoza]. But now these people attack our country and our freedom. If it wasn't for them I would never have had anything to do with guns, and I would still have my right hand. I am trying to train my left hand but it's not the same. I was a cartoonist, you know."—JUAN FRANCISCO LOPEZ, 19-year-old soldier

22

Political hype and propaganda, mainly emanating from the United States, have distorted the public perception of this war, which the U.S. says is happening in "our backyard." Neither Nicaragua nor any of the other countries of Central America are anybody's "backyard."

But the sad history of Central America reveals that since President Monroe's 1823 message to Congress which in later years became known as the "Monroe Doctrine"—the concept of America's "manifest destiny," or plainly stated, what the North American Establishment took to be their "right" to control and exploit the peoples of the region—not only have successive administrations adhered to the Doctrine, they have done everything to ensure that all the countries of the Americas remain directly or indirectly under U.S. control.

> "They seem destined to plague [Latin] America to misery in the name of liberty."—SIMON BOLIVAR, 1829

In reality they have particularly wanted the six Central American countries to remain satellites, as much as Soviet Russia has insisted that the countries of Eastern Europe remain within her empire.

> "I don't see why we need to stand by and watch a country go communist due to the irresponsibility of its own people."—HENRY KISSINGER, June 27, 1970, urging funds for C.I.A. covert action to stop the election of Salvador Allende in Chile.

In January 1984 Henry Kissinger, as chairman of the Bipartisan Commission on Central America:

> "refused to rule out military intervention in Nicaragua which he said had become a haven for communist intelligence operations.—BBC World Service, January 15th.

Until the Reagan administration began to promote the idea that the "Sandinista Communists" were about to sweep up the isthmus and take over the southern states, few knew much about Nicaragua except that it grew coffee, bananas and had had a dictator. "What was his name?"...and..."Didn't they have a revolution down there?"

Even the supposedly all-knowing Ronald Reagan observed with surprise after a whistle stop tour of the region "they're all individual countries down there!"[1] Such was the knowledge of the man most responsible for the war. The remark was made to the press corps on his way back to the U.S. after just five days during which he visited Brazil, Colombia, Costa Rica and Honduras, where he held a mini Central American summit.

The summit was to have taken place in Costa Rica but had to be switched to Honduras owing to the attendance of General Rios Montt, at the time the "born-again" leader of Guatemala. Guatemala has possibly the worst human rights record of any country in Central America, and the Costa Ricans, on the whole a peaceful and democratic nation, held the Guatemalan military in such contempt that they refused to permit the general to enter their country.

"I think they've been given a bum rap,"[2] said Reagan of his new-found friends the Guatemalan military into whose hands Guatemala had been delivered in 1954 by the C.I.A. and who between 1966 and '76 murdered at least 20,000 indians and peasants.[3]

President Reagan went on to say of his visit: "I went down to find out from them and learn." As a result of this swiftly acquired knowledge, he said, while addressing the European Parliament in 1985: "...Today we see similar Soviet efforts to profit from and stimulate regional conflicts in Central America..." He never got any further. Euro-MPs, contemptuous of his undeclared war, shouted him down and waved placards in support of Nicaragua as they left the chamber in protest. He then tried to have the last word by informing those who remained: "They haven't been there, I have!"

No matter how sincere he may have sounded, that was a lie. According to the United States Embassy in London Ronald Reagan has never been to Nicaragua or El Salvador, his other Central American irritant. The nearest he has been to either country was Honduras for the mini-summit, and he stayed for just one day.

He did not invite a representative from Nicaragua to the summit; one can only assume that he felt that the C.I.A. had told him all he needed to learn about that country.

The first U.S. Military intervention in Nicaragua took place in 1855 when the adventurer William Walker invaded on behalf of the Nicaraguan Liberals, in order to win the country for them from the Conservatives. But having succeeded in his mission, he decided that rather than hand it back to his employers he would keep the country for himself, and assumed the title of President. Walker re-established slavery and made English the national language, and his "government" was recognized by Washington. However, he didn't last long and the bitter rivalry between the Conservative and Liberal landed families, which had provided the opportunity for his invasion in the first place and had robbed Nicaragua of stability ever since independence from Spain in 1821, continued.

In 1912 U.S. Marines invaded again, this time to protect the Conservative government of Adolfo Diaz, a more pliable friend than the opposing Liberals. The marines remained until 1926 and, though they were scaled down to a token force of just a few hundred men, their presence confirmed for many Nicaraguans the suspicion that their country was nothing but a colony of the

United States; as indeed it was in all but name. Successive U.S. backed Conservatives acted as little more than the officers of the State Department and U.S. corporate and banking institutions, which had considerable investments in the country.

Within a year the marines returned to help the Conservatives crush an uprising of the "Constitutionalists," who essentially wished a liberal democracy independent of imperial and particularly U.S. control. Though the original revolt was quelled, the Constitutionalists and one of their commanders in particular would not give up the fight.

Augusto Cesar Sandino, the illegitimate son of a coffee planter from Niquinohomo, a small village which lies in the shadow of the Masaya Volcano, had traveled extensively throughout Central America and upon his return from Mexico in 1926 formed his own autonomous brigade to fight alongside the Constitutionalists. Sandino had a vision of a really free, democratic Nicaragua. He despised both the Liberals and Conservatives who mouthed platitudes about democracy while constantly being subservient to the U.S., and eventually he felt the same way about Jose Maria Moncada, the Leader of the Constitutionalist Army. Sandino considered that in the end he too sold out to the "Yankees" in agreeing to a truce during which both sides would disarm in exchange for U.S.-sponsored elections the following year; the U.S. insisting that, whatever the outcome of the elections, the Conservative Adolfo Diaz would remain president. "As a Nicaraguan" said Sandino, "I had a duty to protest." He refused to cooperate and took to the mountains with his men, whom he revealed had elevated him to the rank of general.

For the next six years, supported by growing numbers of peasants, Sandino and his mercurial Army in Defense of National Sovereignty waged a guerrilla war to oust the now more than six thousand U.S. Marines and bring independence and democracy to his country.

On December 22, 1927, as part of the truce that Moncada had agreed to, the United States promoted and signed the Cuadra-Pasos-Muro treaty, ordering the creation of the *Guardia Nacional,* and on January 1, 1933, confirmed Anastasio Somoza Garcia as its commander in chief. Somoza was born in San Marcos, a neighboring village to Sandino's birthplace. He was also the son of a coffee planter, but there any similarlity between the two men ended. He was a man who always had an eye out for the main chance and had inherited many of the characteristics of his great-uncle, Bernabé Somoza, Nicaragua's most notorious bandit who had attempted unsuccessfully to take control of the country in the 1840's and was hung for his trouble. Obviously, meglomania is genetic.

The Guardia were intended to be a non-political national force which would slowly take over the policing of the country from the marines and secondarily combat Sandino should that be necessary.

Some military writers assert that Sandino's was the first real guerrilla war and that his tactics formed the basis of subsequent guerrilla strategy worldwide. Whether this is indeed so is debatable but the war certainly produced other strategies that were to echo down the twentieth century.

On July 17, 1928, after two days of fighting in the northern town of Ocotal, Sandino had a detachment of marines and a number of Guardia pinned down in their barracks when, in an attempt to wipe him out, U.S. war planes carried out the first aerial dive bombing of civilian targets in the history of warfare.

> "And so, General Sandino was in the town with some of his men. At eleven in the morning two planes came. They flew around and then they left. But at two in the afternoon five planes came back, right, and then these planes started bombing all of this area.... Boom, Boom, Boom! When everything was over we came here. All the dead were lying around and they were taken away in ox carts; there were about a hundred of them. Me and two other boys, we found a bomb in the ground that hadn't exploded, we tried to dig it up, but one of the Yankees came and said, "No, no, no don't touch it" and he gave us a dollar each for finding it!
>
> And then General Sandino said, The Americans would have to go to bring peace to Nicaragua. If not the struggle would go on. And then, all the Yankees left. But the struggle did go on, until now, for all of my life."—JOSE IGNACIO MEJIA

The U.S. considered Sandino so dangerous to their interests that for some time they refused to even admit that there was a war or that he and his army were anything more than bandits.

> "We are no more bandits than was Washington. If the American public had not become so calloused to justice and to the elemental rights of mankind, it would not so easily forget its own past when a handful of ragged soldiers marched through the snow, leaving blood tracks behind them, to win liberty and independence. If their consciences had not become so dulled by their scramble for wealth, Americans would not so easily forget the lesson that, sooner or later, every nation, however weak, achieves freedom, and that every abuse of power hastens the destruction of the one who wields it."—AUGUSTO CESAR SANDINO[4]

I wonder if President Reagan or any of his advisers have ever read that while trying to "listen and learn." I somehow doubt it, since Sandino's words are as poignant today as when they were uttered in 1928.

By 1932 Congress was losing heart and wanted the boys to come home; Sandino was leading them a merry dance and their casualties were rising with, it appeared, no hope of defeating him. With no more marines in Nicaragua, they argued, what would Sandino have to fight for.

So in early 1932 the last combat marines left and Juan Bautista Sacasa, a Liberal, was elected President. Sacasa had agreed with the U.S. that he would negotiate a peace with Sandino, whose revolution had been seriously affecting U.S. investments in the country, and assured them that the Guardia would remain a non-political force. He also agreed that Anastasio Somoza would continue as its commander in chief.

Congress had been right in one respect. With no more marines in Nicaragua and Sarcasa's assurances regarding the *Guardia Nacional,* Sandino signed the peace treaty in February 1933, which brought an end to the war and compensated his men, who were to lay down their arms, by providing a tract of land in the Rio Coco valley where they could start a cooperative. But, doubting the sincerity of the ever-ambitious Somoza, Sandino insisted that a provision be added that would permit him to retain a personal armed body-guard of one hundred Sandinistas, as they were already known.

Sandino's suspicions proved justified. Somoza increasingly used the National Guard to cement his political power-base and, although Sandino honored his side of the peace agreement, he did not cease his political activity; the fighting may have been over, but Nicaragua still lacked much that Sandino passionately believed she deserved. To Somoza any talk of political reform, particularly control of his ever-more oppressive Guardia, was a threat that had to be met with force.

By late February 1934 Sandinistas were being harassed constantly and clashes with the Guardia became regular occurrences. On February 21st Sandino returned to the capital, Managua, demanding negotiations with President Sacasa for reforms which would clip Somoza's political wings. That night, as he left a meeting at the Presidential Palace, he was arrested on Somoza's orders and, along with his brother and two officers, was bundled off to the U.S.-built airfield which lay on the outskirts of the city. There they were unceremoniously shot dead, signaling the beginning of the 45-year Somoza dynasty.

Directed, trained and financed by the U.S. the National Guard continued as both a proxy force protecting North American interests and as the Somozas' private army. As a family dictatorship the Somozas were as repressive and cruel as any in Latin America. Together with United States corporations they kept the majority of Nicaraguans in poverty for over fifty years. It benefited both parties; U.S. corporations made money out of the land and its cheap peasant labor and the Somozas grew fat from similar exploitation and out-and-out theft. They stole vast areas of agricultural land and took control of whole sectors of manufacturing industry and merchandising.

By the sixties the Somozas were more like chairmen of the board than presidents. They owned the Lanica Airline and a shipping line, they had sugar, alcohol, livestock, cigarette and cigar factories and refineries, coffee, cotton and cattle estates in eight provinces, and the national cement company which produced the paving blocks for all Nicaragua's roads, plus the company that sold the numerous Mercedes-Benzes to the rich. And, of course, they could dip into the national till at will because they owned the National Bank.

After the 1972 earthquake which completely razed the center of Managua—except, ironically, the Bank of America and Intercontinental Hotel buildings—and left 20,000 dead, Anastasio the Second stole $80 million which had been sent by the international community for the relief and reconstruction of the devastated city and its people.

Resistance to the Somozas over the years was slow to galvanize, partly because of the speed and ruthlessness of both the first Somoza and his heirs. Opponents and critics of whatever political affiliation were culled mercilessly one by one as they came to *El Jefe's* attention. But every barbaric torture imaginable—the slicing off of testicles while the victim was conscious, the dropping of victims from helicopters into the Masaya Volcano, rape and sodomy of children and adults alike—failed to smother their defiance and engendered greater determination to finish what Sandino had begun. In 1961 the F.S.L.N. (Sandinista National Liberation Front) was founded under his black and red banner creating a cohesive body which was to challenge politically, and in the seventies militarily, the Somozas. They came from all walks of life—peasants, urban industrial workers, the middle class, and some, like Daniel and Humberto Ortega, sons whose fathers had fought with Sandino. Their ideology, drawn from many forms of political and social thought, matured into something uniquely Nicaraguan—Sandinismo:

"You cannot say it's Marxism, or Leninism, or Communism. It is, how can I say, Creole Socialism."—XABIER GAROSTIAGA, Panamanian Economist

When Ronald Reagan took office in January, 1981, he did so having regenerated within the American people a wholly unreasonable fear of the Soviet Union and its so-called Communism, thus justifying the largest military budget the world had ever known.

"It is time for us to start a build-up, a rebuilding of the military might of America and it is time for us to build that to the point where no other nation on earth will ever dare raise a hand against us."—RONALD REAGAN, 1980

However, the policy had a problem; in order to fully justify the expenditure there had to be an enemy, more importantly, one that could be beaten with little or no actual risk to the United States. Clearly a confrontation with the Soviet Union was out of the question, even an indirect one. So the administration began to cast about for "enemies" that could be beaten, and Nicaragua in their eyes fit the bill (as did Grenada, but that's another story). An impoverished country of barely three million people who had recently undergone a revolution, it would be easy to sell to the American people as "communist." Furthermore, because of its proximity to the U.S., real Soviet military involvement was impossible, and thus, the administration must have reasoned, they would crush the Sandinistas and be able to turn to the American people and say, "You see, it works, we beat communism yet again." While Reagan hasn't achieved that particular objective, nor is he likely to, he did invoke the same sentiments during the 1984 election campaign when he said: "Not one inch of territory in the world went Communist during our watch."

Subsequently, employing the language of the bully, he further demeaned the office of President when during his State of the Union address in 1985 he talked of making the Sandinistas cry "Uncle!"

"What we have in Nicaragua is a revolution that was fought, literally with our approval. The United States stayed back. And any time there's a revolution, there are factions, all of whom are opposed to the government that they're rebelling against, and they joined together. They promised all the other countries in the Americas—Canada, the United States, all the Latin American countries—they promised that their goal was a democratic government, with free elections, pluralism, free labor unions, human rights observed, freedom of speech and religion and so forth.

"When the revolution was over this country, under the previous administration, immediately went in with aid, more financial aid to the new government of Nicaragua than had been given in 40 years to the previous government of Nicaragua; but then saw them do exactly what Castro did in Cuba after he won the revolution—his people won the revolution. The one faction, the Sandinistas, that faction eliminated all other participants in the revolution.

"Some were exiled. Some had to flee the country. Many were jailed. And they drove them out and then they made it plain, as Castro did in 1959, that they intended a Marxist-Leninist state. And they violated every promise they'd made to the Organization of American States.

"Now the people that are so-called 'Contras,' that are fighting against this, are veterans of the revolution. They are not remnants of the previous government trying to get back into power. Many of them were imprisoned themselves by the previous dictator. And they're demanding a restoration of the democratic goals of the revolution. And we feel obligated to support them."—RONALD REAGAN, Press Conference, April 30, 1985

It all sounds so plausible and, more important, concerned, doesn't it. It also implies a moral "right," a growingly worrisome feature of successive administrations at which none has been more adept than Reagan's.

In spite of the appalling use of the English language and terrible syntax, which the eminent psychologist Dr. Oliver Sacks attributes to rapid senile decay,[5] the statement is worth examining since it contains, firstly, a considerable amount of misinformation and, secondly, represents many of the arguments which Reagan uses to justify his war against the people of Nicaragua.

He begins by saying that the "revolution was fought, literally with our approval, the United States stayed back." Such incredible paternalism surely should have no place in twentieth-century foreign affairs. Does he really see the U.S. as a reflection of his own manufactured image? The Hollywood Lawman dispensing approval and therefore bestowing legitimacy. Does the United States have the right to interfere in the affairs of Nicaragua, or any other nation for that matter, even supposing what the President was saying was true? It does not, not under any law, either American or international.

During those fifty years that the U.S. underwrote the Somoza dynasty with long-term military assistance and loans which ordinary Nicaraguan people paid for with their lives, the President's "democratic goals" were never mentioned. On the contrary, a State Department briefing document prepared for President Roosevelt actually said of the first Somoza, "He may be a son-of-a-bitch, but at least he's ours"; an observation that applied equally to his heirs. The President carefully avoided any mention of this, or that it was only in the latter days of the revolution that President Carter suspended U.S. military assistance to the last Somoza and then only when it became obvious that he could not survive the revolution.

So the history and truth of the current situation is considerably at odds with the Reagan version.

"We do not talk to say something, but to obtain a certain effect."—JOSEPH GOEBBELS, Minister of Propaganda, Nazi Germany

When nations and their leaders disseminate propaganda, whether for internal or external consumption, truth is irrelevant. Once a statement has been made, especially if one supposedly as knowledgeable and honest as a president makes it, it has its desired effect; and if it is repeated often enough the statement is taken to be fact, no matter how many declarations of the truth may appear subsequently to contradict it ("If enough mud gets slung, some of it is bound to stick"). So it is with the defamation of the Sandinistas and the lauding of the Contras.

The Contras (short for *Contra Revolutionarios* [Counter Revolutionaries]) are in fact a C.I.A. army and were initially financed by them when they deemed it necessary to attempt to destroy the fledgling independent state by starting a "covert" war.[6]

"I suppose that if you were Samuel Johnson you would assume that covert meant completely unknown, unprovable and that was originally the idea. We made it clear that we had such policies and operations and that since we had them nobody could know what they were. But it is vital to be able to interpret events in a way that is suitable to get public support for official policy and since the events that one is asking support for are so contrary to the public interest and to the interests of most other nations, what one must do is reinterpret them.... What you have to do is say that a covert action is simply a necessary instrument of policy. But since you also have to gain public support for some covert actions as they become known, we've now invented the 'overt covert' action!

"Nicaragua was originally covert, but became known...so Mr. Reagan began openly talking about his covert action and saying that this is a necessary thing. He was comparing the former Somoza National Guardsmen who were on record as having committed all sorts of atrocities when they were in office, with the Freedom Fighters of various other countries he espouses. In order to be able to talk about this, what you have to do is create an overt discussion of a covert operation. This means you are able to make your case publicly while at the same time denying the public—because it is still covert you insist—any actual knowledge of what is going on...they cannot even know what we are doing but they do know that we are doing it.... That's covert overt! A nice sophistication. Goebbels would have been proud."—TOM GERVASI, Director, Center for Military Research

Creating, or using, an existing armed group as a proxy force to fight a covert war is not a new phenomenon. U.S. agencies used the same technique in Laos and continue to do so in Kampuchea, Chad and Angola. The Soviet Union does it in Iran.

On July 19, 1979, when Nicaraguans took control of their country, some ten thousand National Guards and Somoza officials fled to Honduras beyond Nicaragua's northern border. A few organized into bands which began terrorizing villages in the border areas in the name of Somoza and his

Nicaragua. But they lacked the resources necessary to form themselves into an army.[7]

Possibly because of his Hollywood background, which sees the world in childish black-and-white terms with none of the subtlety of real life, Reagan was attracted to these bandits. They fit well into his limited understanding of international affairs which is divided only into "Us" and "Communists" and into his administration's need for an enemy. Since the Sandinistas espoused socialistic ideals, in Reagan's simplistic view of the world they must be, as he said in his press interview, "Marxist-Leninist." Something incidentally that the F.S.L.N. has never claimed.

> "Oh, I'm quite confident that Reagan has never looked at Marx other than maybe a statue! No, I think that on that level the American leadership is quite illiterate when it comes to matters of political ideology, and I think very few people who've been in responsible positions of power in the United States have any kind of serious understanding of Marxist or Leninist ideology. There's extremely little understanding on the part of the top leadership, they operate with very abstract generalizations about the nature of nationalism, about the nature of Communism, about the kinds of political movements that exist in the world, and they see them in very stereotyped forms that fail to do justice to their particular quality. I do think it's a characteristic of the imperial mind generally that it tends to view the problem of relationships as one of exerting effective control and therefore it doesn't have very much sensitivity to what it is it's seeking to control. In the case of Nicaragua, for instance, the label Marxism-Leninism that even liberal media have attached to this revolution—*The New York Times* is as guilty as *The Wall Street Journal*—it's just not accurate because what the Nicaraguans have brought together I think is a kind of radical nationalism with a socialist Marxist element influencing its economic policy but also with a very strong influence from liberation theology which has if anything gained in significance since the Sandinistas have come to power. And to miss that as a special element of bringing together a religious tradition with radical politics is to miss the essence of what it is that holds the people basically behind this revolutionary process and makes it very different than what happened in Cuba two decades earlier...."—PROFESSOR RICHARD FALK, Princeton University

In 1981, when Reagan took office, he secretly ordered that the Contras be formed into a proper army with the sole purpose of destroying the Sandinistas. The C.I.A. obeyed, bringing the various bandit groups together under the umbrella of the F.D.N. (Nicaraguan Democratic Force). In November 1981 he further authorized $19.95 million to the Contras to carry out "covert actions" again Nicaragua. At the same time the C.I.A. established military training camps,[8] some actually in the U.S. in violation of U.S. law. Contra bases were set up on Honduran territory, presumably with the knowledge of that country's government, and soon the whole border area was bristling with all the paraphernalia of modern military support. As a result of the C.I.A. training and financial backing more ex-National Guards joined their number and acts of terrorism became commonplace.

At the end of 1982 the C.I.A. directed the restructuring of the F.D.N. military commands, together with the formation of a Political Directorate.

Reagan states:

"...the people that are so-called Contras...are veterans of the revolution."

I suppose it depends on what your interpretation of "a veteran" is, but it can never be argued that the Contras fought to overthrow Somoza. Eleven of the seventeen people who make up the Political Directorate of the F.D.N. are ex-Somosistas and 46 of the 48 military leaders are ex National Guards.[9]

"My experience as a former rebel leader has convinced me that the F.D.N. cannot contribute to the democratization of Nicaragua. The rebels are in the hands of former National Guardsmen who control the 'contra army,' stifle internal dissent and intimidate or murder those who dare oppose them."— EDGAR CHAMORRO, Non-Somoza ex-member of the F.D.N.

It is true that a few of the Contras, a very few, were veterans of anti-Somoza forces. Their leader was Eden Pastora, who was neither "exiled" nor "driven out." A former commander of the Sandinistas, Comandante Cero as he was known during the war years, had an on/off relationship with his compatriots. He is rich, a flamboyant character who socially had little in common with his F.S.L.N. compatriots. He owned lands in Nicaragua and has business in neighboring Costa Rica. He also envisaged a Sandinista victory as a vehicle for personal gain and power. However, after the victory the members of the newly formed National Directorate, whose task it was to run the country until a government was elected, agreed that if the country were to really make a political turn towards a more democratic and egalitarian society, the example had to come from the top, from the people who had carried the vision of Sandino. It had to be shown that those who were advocating democracy and a fairer distribution of wealth should be the first to practice it; and this was in line with another element so important to their victory, Liberation Theology.

To extricate itself from the legacy of poverty and corruption that had been the hallmark of the Somozas, the members of the National Directorate agreed that no member could own land or property of substance or have business interests overseas; the leaders would practice what they preached. But Pastora would have none of it. He insisted that such policies were proof that the Sandinistas were becoming totalitarian and refused to give his lands over to the state and similarly would not give up his financial interests abroad. Eventually he fled with some of his fighters to Costa Rica where from 1982 he commanded his C.I.A.-financed private army, ARDE, with logistic assistance from the Costa Rican border forces.

However, Pastora did retain some principals from his years with the Sandinistas in that he refused repeated C.I.A. entreaties to unite with the main F.D.N. Contras in Honduras. Lacking support from the population and with morale hitting rock bottom, in June 1986, having achieved nothing except the killing and maiming of hundreds of Nicaraguans, Pastora and the last 500 of his ARDE force laid down their arms and dispersed.

With the Sandinista victory Somoza fled the country, taking with him most of the gold and cash from the National Bank, which he owned, and leaving nothing in the national treasury while the accumulated foreign debt which the Sandinistas inherited was somewhere in the region of $2 billion.

As Reagan pointed out in his press conference, the Sandinistas made promises to the Organization of American States. But contrary to his assertions, they have kept those promises. Elections were held in 1984 and the new National Assembly is made up of representatives from a number of political parties both to the right and left of the Sandinistas. The elections, according to independent foreign observers, were free and fair,[10] and the turnout of 74 percent, of which the Sandinistas got 63 percent, was considerably higher than that which gave Reagan his second term in the same year.

Together with Costa Rica, Nicaragua is the only other country in the Americas to have completely abolished the death penalty. There are few political prisoners, the majority there are former National Guards. The churches are full and freedom of worship is a constitutional right even though many of the current political attacks emanate from the hierarchy of that sector. All of Somoza's lands, together with those of absentee landlords, have been redistributed. Literacy has increased dramatically, public health centers are being built, infant mortality, endemic disease and malnutrition are decreasing.

I suppose it is not surprising that President Reagan never mentions any of those things, nor the fact that a large section of the middle class, private landowners and industrialists are among the staunchest supporters of the revolution; it's not just the peasantry who believe in Sandinismo.

After years of oppression in which 50,000 Nicaraguans were killed, the overthrow of Somoza gave everyone a chance for a better life. But of course the financing and support of the Contras to destroy all of that continues and the lies and deceptions grow.

"We must stand by all our democratic allies. And we must not break faith with those who are risking their lives—on every continent, from Afghanistan to Nicaragua—to defy Soviet-supported aggression....Support for freedom fighters is self-defense, and totally consistent with the O.A.S. and U.N. Charters."—RONALD REAGAN, State of the Union Address, 1985

"The covert war against Nicaragua is one of the most blatant violations of international law, indeed the most fundamental and universally accepted principles of international law, that any great power has ever committed. In particular this war violates the United Nations Charter and the Charter of the Organization of American States, and it is also in violation of customary International law. Because of that, Nicaragua brought a law suit against the United States in the International Court of Justice. The reaction to that law suit really speaks volumes.... The United States walked out of the Court. That's like a gangster refusing to recognize the jurisdiction of a criminal court and turning around and walking away. It's about as compelling an admission of guilt, a confession of wrong-doing as one can imagine."—PAUL REICHLER, International Lawyer, Washington, D.C.

By June 1986, under severe pressure from Ronald Reagan, the United States Congress had voted over $212,000,000 in military aid to the Contras. Money for guns, money for bullets, money for shells and mortars that kill and maim ordinary citizens.

"It just shouldn't happen. There's no excuse for it. I mean we're attacking a people, we're attempting to destroy a government which very clearly has the support of the majority of the people in this country. I mean it's very depressing to me and angers me greatly when I go to the northern border of Nicaragua and talk to a mother who's had three kids hit by a mortar that I know full well my government paid for and encouraged to lob, and then, to look in the house and see the kids' blood on the wall."—HOMER YOST, U.S. Volunteer Worker

"I don't think there's real appreciation in the U.S. Congress of the activities that the Contras are engaged in. The fact that they're engaged in murder and rape and mayhem, in violence against the civilian population, the coffee growers, the farmers, the civilians in that country. Not against the Sandinista army. And what you see is after Congress spent years and years tying conditions to aid to El Salvador to get rid of the stat-run Death Squads that were roaming that country, we now find that it is the United States of America that has introduced the Death Squads into Nicaragua. They're being financed and paid for by the United States Government and they're the ones that are killing the civilian population in Nicaragua."—CONGRESSMAN GEORGE MILLER

In 1984 a young New York Lawyer went to Nicaragua to make an independent investigation into the increasing reports of atrocities allegedly committed by the Contras. The report, entitled *Attacks by the Nicaraguan Contras on the Civilian Population of Nicaragua—Report of a Fact-Finding Mission, September 1984 to January 1985,* is a 141-page document based on nearly 150 sworn affidavits from witnesses and victims of Contra attacks. It makes some of the most sickening reading it is possible to imagine.

"...two independent investigators went to Nicaragua to verify this report—Michael Glennin, a law professor at the University of Cincinnati, former Counsel to the Senate Foreign Relations Committee, and Donald Fox a distinguished lawyer, human rights expert from New York. They were appalled by what they found. They went to the United States Embassy in Managua and spoke with the ambassador, Ambassador Harry Bergold. They told him what they had found. They told him that they were outraged by what was going on with the United States support. They asked the ambassador if the State Department had made any investigation, if the United States Government knew at all about what was happening. Ambassador Bergold responded that U.S. policy is one of intentional ignorance, that *it is the policy of the United States not to know and not to find out what the Contras are doing to the civilian population in Nicaragua.*"—PAUL REICHLER

"Five of them raped me at about five in the evening....they had gang raped me every day. When my vagina couldn't take it anymore, they raped me through my rectum. I calculate that in five days they raped me 60 times."—DIGNA BARREDA DE UBEDA, mother of two, kidnapped by Contras May 1983. (*Attacks by the Nicaraguan Contras on the Civilian Population of Nicaragua—Report of a Fact-Finding Mission, September 1984 to January 1985.*)

"This is not a military base, this is just a small cooperative. When the Contras came there were fifty of us members of the cooperative and about five hundred Contras. They attacked with mortars, rifles, repeating rifles. They destroyed everything. There are children here and women and old people. We fled in the night we lost everything."—Cooperative Sandino, Jinotega

"When we were all in the [bomb] shelter, my mother asked if any of the children were missing, so we called them by their names. Only Suyapa was missing. I went out...then I remembered that I had seen her playing with a hen. I went there and saw her dead. Her face was blown away but I didn't realize it, I didn't even notice the mortaring. I picked her up and ran away like mad. Then I realized that part of her face was missing. I went back to look and found the piece of her face."—CARMEN GUTIERREZ. (*Attacks by the Nicaraguan Contras on the Civilian Population of Nicaragua—Report of a Fact-Finding Mission, September 1984 to January 1985*).

"They had already destroyed all that was the cooperative; a coffee drying machine, the two dormitories for the coffee cutters, the electricity generators, seven cows, the plant, the food warehouse...there was one boy about 15 years old who was retarded and suffered from epilepsy. We had left him in a bomb shelter...when we returned...we saw...that they had cut his throat, then they cut open his stomach and left his intestines hanging out on the ground like a string....They did the same to Juan Corrales who had already died from a bullet in the fighting. They opened him up and took out his intestines and cut off his testicles."—DOROTEO TINOCO VALDIVIA. (*Attacks by the Nicaraguan Contras on the Civilian Population of Nicaragua—Report of a Fact-Finding Mission, September 1984 to January 1985*).

44

"Once inside the town, the Contra force set about destroying it's key civilian and economic installations.

"The state-owned lumber mill and processing plant in Barrio Sandino, which produced an estimated 14,000 ft. of processed wood daily, was attacked by machine guns, mortars and grenades. Incendiary bombs were then used to set fire and destroy a plane, the saw and conveyor belt, the fork-lift, the lathe and the mechanic shop including a small truck, a pick-up truck, two caterpillar tractor motors, one tractor, the electrical system, the welding apparatus and the stock of tools. The total economic damage was estimated at between 10 and 15 million Cordobas (approx. $200,000) and an estimated 250 persons were left jobless."—PETER OLSON, U.S. citizen, witness to attack on Ocotal, June 1984. (*Attacks by the Nicaraguan Contras on the Civilian Population of Nicaragua—Report of a Fact-Finding Mission, September 1984 to January 1985).*

In January 1984 the National Bipartisan Commission on Central America published its findings. Chaired by Henry Kissinger, it was intended to be Ronald Reagan's blueprint for future foreign policy in the region. The report played heavily on the rhetoric of the Cold War and constantly cited Nicaragua as the reason for all the region's problems. According to the report Nicaragua has a Marxist/Leninist regime and is an agent of the Soviet Union and Cuba.

"They are nobody's agents. They are strictly Nicaraguan Nationalists. Their ideology is eclectic and borrows from many ideologies and systems around the world, but above all else it is what they say it is—Sandinismo. It is uniquely Nicaraguan and, frankly, I think that's something that the United States ought to be encouraging, not trying to stamp out."—PAUL REICHLER

Dr. Kissinger insists that Nicaragua represents a threat to the United States:

"Now there is the added threat of an entire new set of problems posed by Nicaragua. It already serves as a base of subversion, through overland infiltration of people and supplies, that can affect the entire region, Panama included. Panama is gradually assuming full responsibility for the security of the Canal; this means that any threat to the political security of that country and to the maintenance of its friendly relations with the United States automatically constitutes a strategic threat."[11]

Apart from the fact that it is quite ridiculous to suggest that Nicaragua, with a population of 3 million and an economy that is in ruins owing to the Somoza legacy and America's "covert war," could possibly represent a strategic threat to the United States, the Kissinger statement yet again demonstrates that U.S. thinking regarding the region has changed not one jot in the past century. President Monroe would be pleased. The threat that, in adherence to the concepts of the Doctrine, they do represent is that of example. An economically and politically successful independent Nicaragua might make others in the region reconsider the imperial nature of their relationships with the United States. But balance sheets and Manifest Destiny preclude that ever being mentioned directly by the Administration.

"Nicaragua represents no threat to the United States unless you make up threats about the Sandinistas taking over the United States, taking over Mexico. Or if you make up threats about them sinking the American Navy, about them destroying the American shipping lanes. This is a country that can't keep its trucks repaired. This is a country where if it moves at all, it generally moves on foot or broken-down truck—and you make up scenarios about the Soviets putting in ICBM's (Intercontinental Ballistic Missiles). There's no way in the world that the United States would stand for that for five minutes. The Soviets know it. The Nicaraguans know it and we know it. But that's the basis on which we keep killing people in that country, by creating threats that are simply non-existent. Let's remember the Sandinistas haven't invaded anybody. They've been invaded by the Hondurans, they've been invaded by the Americans. For all their military build-up which troubles this Congress and this administration, they haven't invaded anybody. They've been invaded by the strongest military power in the world."—Congressman George Miller

When stories began to leak that the United States government was behind the creation and financing of the Contras and that yet again the C.I.A. was involved in another "covert war" the administration was stuck to find a good excuse. While they wished to be rid of the Sandinistas, the "Communist Threat" groundwork had not been fully laid and to admit at this stage that overthrow was the actual intent would raise embarrassing questions of legality. A good interim story had to be found, so after various denials, it was admitted that certain funds had gone to the Contras to help them to "interdict a flow of weapons from Nicaragua to the rebels in El Salvador." No one bothered to examine the logistical impossibilities which made this explanation quite ridiculous. Nicaragua and El Salvador do not share a common land border. Honduras, which is hostile to both and is America's forward base in the region, lies between them. The only other possible route is across the Gulf of Fonseca, but just how this flow of arms was supposed to cross this wild stretch of water which is constantly patrolled by the U.S. Navy and covered by some of the most sophisticated radar equipment imaginable, not to mention the nightly aerial surveillance flights, was never questioned.

The Gulf has been sewn up since 1981 by United States hardware when Secretary of State Alexander Haig proclaimed that the string of small islands and outcrops in the Gulf were henceforth "Reagan's Line" and "Communism" would stop there; rather like the Seventeenth Parallel in Vietnam where two decades earlier Robert McNamara had proposed building an electrified fence across that country—"McNamara's Line"—actually cutting the North from the South to "sanitize the country from the disease of communism." However, no flow of weapons from Nicaragua to El Salvador was ever "interdicted" and the only hardware ever found was planted by the C.I.A.

When the war in Vietnam ended, about half a million M16 assault rifles, the standard infantryman's weapon, were left by the departing U.S. forces. The army, being bound by paperwork, had the serial numbers of all these guns and when the Administration needed to produce evidence that, in Haig's words, "with Cuban coordination, the Soviet Bloc, Vietnam, Ethiopia and radical Arabs are furnishing at least several hundred tons of military equipment to the Salvadoran leftist insurgents,"[12] they were able to point to a consignment of M16s allegedly "interdicted" in El Salvador and show that, yes, the serial numbers indeed matched those of weapons left in Vietnam, and so the

Secretary of State's accusation must have been correct. What, however, was carefully avoided was any mention of a rather important link in the chain between Vietnam and El Salvador which if revealed would have told quite a different story.

In 1975, Samuel Cummings, one of the world's oldest and most successful private arms dealers, bought a consignment of the abandoned M16s from the Vietnamese. As the freighter carrying them left Haiphong harbor and entered international waters it was intercepted by the U.S. Navy. The cargo was confiscated and consigned to U.S. "Sterile Stocks"—sterile being a National Security term for weapons whose history cannot be traced. It was these M16s that were produced as "evidence." Yes, they had come from Vietnam, but via a C.I.A. Sterile Store in the U.S.[13]

Since this other side to the story was not made public, the financing of the Contras under the guise of "intendiction" was for a while justified.

> "I don't think there is any mystery about it any more. This administration is looking for the eradication and the removal of the Sandinista Government in Nicaragua...that is the only intent that they have ever had....There is nothing, nothing that the Sandinistas can do to satisfy Ronald Reagan, he wants their removal from that country and he has never, never taken a single signal and suggested that it was the beginning, that it was a start of the process towards peaceful resolution."—CONGRESSMAN GEORGE MILLER

Until June of 1984 the Contras had never fought the Nicaraguan army. Instead they were constantly routed by volunteer militiamen. None of the militia are conscripted—all are volunteers. They are ordinary men and women who spend from three to six months away from their families in bases along the Honduran or Costa Rican borders.

> "Right now, the Contras are an organization that are directed by the Government of the United States. They don't want us to be successful. They don't want us to survive. For fifty-odd years we lived under U.S. domination and so with this revolution the general population rose up and were successful. We will defend that victory. We have decided that we do not want the U.S. to rule us...and we are in the right!"—MILITIAMAN, Cooperative Sandino, Jinotega, March 1985

Up to November of 1983 the Contras raided all through the lonely stretch along the border with Honduras. They raped, kidnapped and murdered peasants whose only crime was that they wanted to live in peace. Now everyone has gone. The land lies uncared for, coffee plants being smothered by wild tropical growths. But the land is back under Sandinista control. Most of the men and women are militia. There were about fifty of them, all ages, peasants, factory hands, office workers—ordinary Nicaraguans.

"President Reagan, I would like him to come down here. I would like him to see the country, the people. I would like him to see the patience of the peasants, the workers. We are all peasants and workers. We don't come up here for money, to get a house or a car. We are here for our people, so that our people can live in peace and freedom."—MILITIAMAN, Macarali, 1 km. from the Honduran border

Their graffiti reads: After 50 years Sandino Lives—They shall not pass. Out of the fifty at Macarali, 11 had been killed in two months. Casualties since 1981 are in excess of 32,000 people.

"I would say that on balance previous administrations have seen that the conflicts in the Middle East have indigenous roots. As the conflicts unfold they may draw in the super powers but that the origins of the conflicts are more indigenous and the super-power rivalry is a kind of overlay. Reagan during his campaign for President in 1980 said, in an off-hand moment, that were the Soviet Union not involved in Third World conflicts, there would be no Third World conflicts. But this is taking his perception perhaps to an extreme, that the Soviet Union is behind all of the turmoil in the Third World. Assuming that that was an exaggerated expression of belief that he has I think when you apply that to the Middle East, you look at places like Lebanon or the Palestinian conflict and you don't see that they grow out of historical roots in the Middle East, but you tend to look at the super-power rivalry as the main aspect of these conflicts. So in a place like Lebanon, the Palestinians become surrogates of the Soviet Union; or the Syrians, who when they first went into Lebanon were welcomed by the Americans as a stabilizing force—in Reagan's view they were there as pawns of the Soviet Union. And correspondingly the Israelis emerge as the ally of the West in this confrontation with the Soviets. The net effect is to badly skew the analysis that precedes the making of policy, i.e., when you get the definitions all wrong, you end up with wrong policy."—WILLIAM QUANDT, Senior Fellow, The Brookings Institution

LEBANON

"A different way of dying"

"It's a Chicago gang war. Each faction has its War Lord. There are the War
Lords, their militias and the people. The people have had enough of the war
and enough of politics."—Journalist

"In Lebanon, politics has nothing to do with the truth."—Aid Official

"It's urban renewal. Only it's done rather viciously and sometimes they don't move the people out first."—American Aid Worker

"In Lebanon we have extended families. So even when the shelling is not too close we are anxious because one of our relatives in the next street may have been killed."—Resident, The Green Line

"Israel is Orwell. But Beirut is Blade Runner. This is the 21st century. This is not anarchy—this is beyond anarchy."—EDDIE TISE, Sound Recordist

With most conflicts, past and present, it is possible to sift through the debris of history and by examination determine "who struck the first blow." Invariably one can see that one of the protagonists exceeded the limits of civilized behavior, abandoned diplomacy and political realism, refused to accept compromise and regressed to archaic beliefs such as "Might Is Right." No single event or decision happens in isolation; there are always other actors in the conflict, often on the sidelines, who could have helped alter the course of events and avoided the escalation into war. For example, some argue that by its policy of appeasement, Britain simply encouraged Hitler's ambitions, and had she taken a different line Nazi Germany's ambitions might have been nipped in the bud. Of course, such wisdom comes easy with hindsight, but in many cases it holds true and it is therefore possible to argue that war in all its forms can be avoided if only the one who can be identified as having "struck the first blow" hadn't sunk so low, or others who might have been able to alter the course of history had not simply sat on the sidelines.

But all of this is contradicted by Lebanon. That it should sink into the morass of civil war that now threatens to drown it somehow seems to have been an inevitability.

Lebanon isn't really a country, a nation state. Rather, it is a collection of fiefdoms, radiating out from Mount Lebanon, each of a distinct religious identity, and each contained within specific geographical boundaries.

With the defeat of the Ottoman empire in 1918 the European allies divided the spoils of war; to France went the Ottoman territories of Mount Lebanon and Syria. The League of Nations vested in France a mandate to govern these territories and in 1920, by expanding the old borders to the east of the Bek'ka Valley into Ottoman Syria and south to include the centuries-old ports of Tyre and Sidon, they created the boundaries of Greater Lebanon that exist to this day. In 1926 it was declared a constitutional Republic uniting for the first time the numerous religious, or confessional, groups under one flag and with one parliament.

More than 780,000 people deeply divided along confessional lines—Christians, being Maronite, Greek Orthodox, Greek Catholic, Protestant and various eastern Christian followers, and Muslims of the Sunni, Shi'ite and Druze confessions—were crammed into this tiny country roughly a quarter of the size of Switzerland. Each group had its traditional leading family who were not unlike the feudal landowners of Europe in that they maintained their power through the unquestioning loyalty of their followers. Indeed, loyalty to the landowning family, and therefore their sect, was and still is an obligation from birth; if you were born on the slopes of Mount Lebanon your allegiance was probably to the Maronite Christians, in the Shuf Mountains it was to the Druze, and so on. Landowning family names that are synonymous with today's conflict go back in some cases hundreds of years. Jumblat, Karami, Franjieh, and Salam pepper current news stories, together with the comparatively new names that rose to power through the professions: Edde, Chamoun, Khoury, and Gemayel. It is these families and their followers who are the war lords and militias of today.

Not only is it impossible to determine who struck the first blow but it is also impossible to say when it was struck, since sporadic feuding between the various groups goes back centuries. But it would be far too easy and simplistic to explain away all of Lebanon's problems by saying that it is a war between Christians and Muslims. It would also be quite wrong to suggest, as many have, particularly in the mass media, that it was all the fault of outside, non-Lebanese forces such as the Palestinians, or the Israelis, the Syrians, or indeed the super powers. For in truth it is a complicated combination of all of these factors, with one other element which is almost exclusive to Lebanon.

Many of the war lords, particularly the newer names, are in fact no better than the Chicago gangsters of the twenties. They are completely ruthless and in many cases their rise to power has been achieved not by politicking or even something as simple as ballot rigging, which of course has happened, but by murder. And there therefore is the other factor that makes Lebanon's war unique and beggars description. It is a gang war that is fought with heavy modern weapons behind a mask of righteous sectarianism at untold cost to ordinary Lebanese of all confessions.

In 1943, after considerable pressure from the British, the Free French reluctantly gave Lebanon its independence. The majority of the problems that led to the civil war can be dated to the constitution, drawn up under the French, which attempted to make all confessions feel that they were fairly represented in government, and which was manifest in the 1943 National Pact. Under the terms of the pact the distribution of governmental posts among the confessions was supposed to be representative of the population's confessional breakdown. But this distribution was based on census figures taken in 1932. At that time, according to the census, there were six Christians to every five Muslims and the predominant sects within the broad groupings were the Maronite Christians and the Sunni Muslims. Thus the National Pact gave the presidency to a Maronite, the premiership to a Sunni and the presidency of the Chamber of Deputies to a Shi'ite with other posts in the government and Chamber to represent the six to five Christian majority. What this system actually achieved was the constitutional vesting of real power in the Maronites.

No population remains static and Lebanon's is no exception. It grew rapidly after 1943. But such was the desire, particularly of the Maronites, to retain their political dominance, that no government since has dared carry out another census for fear of what their eyes could tell them was the truth. While all agree that the 1932 census showed 402,363 Christians to 383,180 Muslims, the population has since more than quadrupled. Whereas the current breakdown estimates about 1,350,000 Christians, the Moslem population has shot up to at least 2,050,000.[1] And therein lies the seed of the current problem.

A very rich powerful Christian minority still has a six to five control in parliament over a demoralized Muslim majority who, if the figures are correct—and it appears that they are—outnumber the Christians almost two to one. Over 50 percent are poor Shi'ites and nearly 50 percent of them are under 25 with few job prospects despite their often high level of academic qualification. Into this clearly sensitive and confused situation came another factor which was to be the catalyst.

In 1948 the newly created state of Israel annexed areas of Galilee and Jordan, areas which were formally Palestine. Thousands of Palestinians were expelled, often at gunpoint, and herded across the borders into Jordan, Syria and Lebanon. Following the 1967 war in which Israel occupied the territory along the West Bank of the Jordan, thousands more poured into the refugee camps which were mushrooming around the poorest sections of Lebanon's town and cities. These stateless refugees, whose numbers were in excess of 350,000, were the beginnings of the Palestinian Liberation Organization.

The belief grew within the Palestinian community both in and out of the camps that if they were to have their homeland, they would have to fight for it themselves, for there appeared to be an unwillingness in the Arab world to pay anything other than lip-service to their cause. Indeed, the continuation of the Palestinian problem served the Arab world, for though Israeli reprisals against the P.L.O. often happened in their nations, they were rarely directed at them, and thus the P.L.O. served in general to concentrate Israeli military action on the Palestinians and not the Arab states. This is not to deny that Israel's various wars did not hurt the Arab states; of course they did, but it was the Palestinians who bore the day-to-day brunt of the Israeli military machine.

By 1969 raids across Israel's northern border in both directions happened regularly and both in south Lebanon and around the refugee camps in Beirut the sight of well trained, armed young Palestinians became commonplace.

The P.L.O. introduced into the Lebanese equation something that hadn't existed before: an armed Muslim force capable of challenging the mainly Christian Lebanese Army and the Kata'ib and Ahrar Christian militias of the Gemayel and Chamoun families. And while conservative Lebanese wanted the Palestinians out, Shi'ite and poor Sunnis, especially in the south and Beirut, sympathized with the Palestinians, whom they saw as equals; people who had been left out of the system. Some Lebanese Muslims in fact joined the P.L.O. thinking that in the end this armed force might help bring about the social and political changes they believed imperative to do away with the inequity and political corruption that was the legacy of the National Pact. By contrast it is not surprising that the conservative Lebanese establishment, particularly the Maronites, viewed the P.L.O. as a threat. Not only did they seem to flout the conservative order of things, they were beginning to draw Israeli reprisals upon Lebanon.

When in 1968 Israeli commandos blew up thirteen airliners on the runway at Beirut Airport, the government took it as a sign that Israel expected them to deal with the P.L.O. This, however, proved to be impossible. The P.L.O. were too strong to be disarmed; neither could they be expelled. Where would they go? They were already stateless.

The following year Colonel Gamal Nasser stepped in to try and cool things down by negotiating the Cairo Agreement, which was intended to regulate relations between the Lebanese government and the Palestinians. In effect what the agreement achieved was to cede sovereignty of much of south Lebanon to the P.L.O., enabling them to continue their battle for a homeland virtually unhindered by Beirut. Clearly this was something that to many Christian Lebanese was completely unacceptable. It spawned a fanatical opposition to the Palestinians—a fanaticism which would fester and culminate, 13 years later, in the barbaric massacre of countless Palestinian civilians.

However, it must be remembered that the Palestinians were not the only problem facing the ruling Christians. By late 1974, as the country teetered, unknowingly, on the brink of civil war, Amal the Shi'ite militia appeared. With the blessing of Iman Musa al Sadr, their political and spiritual leader, Amal stepped into an arena that already contained the armed militias of the Sunnis, the Druze and the Communists. In effect, and again this is part of the confusion of the situation, there were now two distinct areas of trouble brewing at the same time. One: tensions between the P.L.O and the Kata'ib; and two: general Lebanese dissatisfaction with corrupt government and the rise to power of the extremist Maronites. Tempers were high and reason had been abandoned, generosity was forgotten and fear ruled.

Inevitably, Lebanon crashed over the edge in April, 1975, when Kata'ib militiamen massacred 27 Palestinians travelling on a bus through Ayn al Rumaneh, a Christian slum suburb of East Beirut. P.L.O. retaliation was swift and bloody, but the fighting could have ended there. However, the Muslim militias took this slaughter as their cue. The city went mad, spontaneously echoing with automatic weapons fire and shuddering to the thump of heavy artillery. Soon it was physically divided along the "Green Line"; Christians in the east, Muslims in the west.

Following the first outburst, the majority of subsequent fighting was between the emerging Lebanese Muslim militias and the Kata'ib and did not further involve the P.L.O. until December, when they formally entered the conflict. The P.L.O. had no desire to become involved; they had their own war with the Israelis and while there was no love lost between them and the Kata'ib, they didn't believe that it was their fight.

Things changed, however, for two reasons. Firstly, the Palestinians felt they owed a debt to the moslem Lebanese who had supported them in the past and whom they were close to ideologically, and secondly, the slum areas of West Beirut where many of these Lebanese lived surrounded the Palestinian refugee camps and it was here that much of the fighting was taking place.

Battles between the rival militias escalated, and as each side struggled to consolidate territory, a city block at a time, it was the civilians in these areas who began to be the victims. What had begun as a war between militias, each representing factions hoping to make political gains, degenerated into a full-scale sectarian war that in its first twelve months claimed at least 50,000, mainly civilian, lives.[2]

No one, however, could win or stop it. Both sides were entrenched and the Lebanese army, the only legitimate armed force, was impotent to do anything. In April, 1976, the Army broke down along confessional lines, its troops joining militias of their own confession. Still, the Christians were nominally the government and President Franjieh with his allies Chamoun and Gemayel asked the Syrians to intervene to help bring about stability. The move suited the Syrians, who wanted to maintain Lebanon within their sphere of influence. They rocked the Muslim militias and implemented a semblance of a cease-fire. But their job done, they had no desire to leave, much to the annoyance of the Maronites who felt that now that Syria had done the dirty work for them, they could at last control the Muslim movement. As luck would have it for the Syrians, the Arab League stepped in and gave them a mandate to be the "peace keepers," thus legitimizing their presence. They remain today.

The next few years produced a non-peace. The country was not constantly at war, neither was it at peace. Sporadic fighting continued, as often as not between factions of a similar confession. Gemayels' Kata'ib destroyed the Chamoun Ahrar Christian militia and amalgamated the remnants with the Kata'ib into a new group, the Lebanese Forces, also known as the Phalange. On the Muslim side, fighting broke out between the Shi'ite and Sunnis as each vied for supremacy.

Meanwhile the P.L.O. tried to keep order in West Beirut at the same time as their leadership were attempting to establish credibility in the international community in order to try to win allies for a political settlement for their own problems with Israel. In 1981, with the U.S. as brokers, a cease-fire was agreed between the P.L.O. and Israel along the Israeli/Lebanese border.

At last it seemed that there might be hope for an accommodation with Israel, particularly if Arafat could keep his side of the agreement and demonstrate to the world that he still had effective control of his people and was prepared to follow the path of diplomacy.

To the surprise of Prime Minister Begin and especially his Defense Minister, General Ariel Sharon, Arafat did honour the cease-fire, something they neither expected nor, as it transpired, did they want. What they did want was a pretext to invade Lebanon.

"The whole idea was conceived by people who had absolutely no idea what the problem was and how it can be achieved or solved. They were moved by some theories which had no relationship to reality.... I think, the P.L.O. is

probably the last and the least important reason. After all, one whole year
before the invasion, the northern border with Lebanon was quiet, perfectly
quiet...there was not one incident, and this was the result of the ceasefire
agreement...and it worked beautifully. Really, the people up North had
complete safety for a whole year, so the argument that the invasion was
necessitated by the P.L.O. hostility is certainly untrue. Israel had for a long
time ambitions regarding Lebanon; when the war of 1948 ended we were, in
fact, in control of South Lebanon all the way up to the Litani River. We gave
up this territory under the Armistice Agreement, but voices calling for
retaking that area, particularly in order to be able to use the Litani River
water, were heard all along. We know now that Ben-Gurion and Dayan
considered the possibility of invading Lebanon in the fifties so the situation
was just considered ripe for such a move, and in order to justify it
internationally, of course, the arguments for establishing a stable
government in Lebanon was very attractive to many ears, particularly in the
United States. For the people in Israel, of course, the argument of getting
rid of the P.L.O. was another pleasant argument to hear, and for the
Phalangists I think it was quite clear that in order to be able to effectively
rule the country, they wanted to decrease the Islamic or the Muslim
population, and the Palestinians are mostly Muslim. So by getting rid of the
Palestinians they could get rid of half a million Muslims, which might
restore the disturbed balance between Christians and Muslims in Lebanon.
So it was part of a big conception, all of which, of course, was based on
hallucinations, as I said before, because it had absolutely no relation to
reality...none of these big ideas could be implemented. Had the government
listened to our own experts they would have known that it was just day-
dreaming, pipe dreaming, but certainly the whole conception was a very big
conception, having very little to do actually with the presence of the P.L.O.
in Lebanon."—MATTI PELED (Gen. Retd I.D.F.) Professor of Arab Literature,
Tel Aviv University

General Sharon visited Alexander Haig, at the time U.S. Secretary of State,
in Washington and informed him that Israel would invade Lebanon, crush the
P.L.O. and establish a 40-km.-deep, demilitarized zone protecting Israel's
northern border; this after all had been one of Begins election promises. The
fact that the cease-fire was having the same effect, keeping the north of Israel
at peace, was an irritant rather than a blessing to Begin and Sharon.

"I would say that the conventional American view has been that Middle East
stability is best for American interest. Reagan and Haig were revisionists in
this sense—they thought that Israel was such an efficient military machine
and had such a clear plan that perhaps they could do what the Americans
found they were unable to do anywhere in the world, namely score a big win
against a pro-Soviet client. Now the Americans had wanted to do it in
Nicaragua and had failed; they wanted to do it against Khadaffi and it failed
and in a sense the Israelis came along and said, 'We can do it to the P.L.O;

you've already described them as pro-Soviet terrorists. We'll deal them a really tough blow and it'll be over with quickly and it can only have good results.' Now anybody who knew the intricacies of the Middle East situation knew that there were going to be a lot of adverse consequences when the Israelis tried that, but I think the Reagan administration in this early and rather naïve phase was willing to accept this revisionist notion—you can redraw the map in the Middle-East and maybe it'll be a map that we like better."—WILLIAM QUANDT, Senior Fellow, The Brookings Institution

Sharon—whom Alexander Haig describes as "a brawny man who uses his bulk, his extremely loud voice, and a flagrantly aggressive manner, which I suspect he has cultivated for effect, to overwhelm opposition"[3]—had intimated that his solution to the Paltestinian situation, after having crushed the P.L.O., would be to annex Jordan, where by now Palestinians represented about 60 percent of the population, get rid of King Hussein and literally give the country to the Palestinians and be done with them. He also had a fanatical belief, which he had spoken of quite openly, that Israel's military influence extended far beyond the Arab world "to englobe Turkey, Iran, Pakistan and up to Central and North Africa"![4] For years the more hawkish of the Zionists had believed that the only solution to Israel's dealings with its Arab neighbors was to reduce their collective power by in effect somehow Balkanizing the Arab world. Though how they expected they could ever achieve such madness is a mystery, for despite their famed military expertise there are at present slightly less than 2 million Jews living in Israel. By contrast they are surrounded by some 200 million Arabs.

Whatever the long-term schemes, they would begin with an invasion of Lebanon. There had already been contact with the Maronites, who of course would be quite happy for the Israelis to do what they could never do, namely drive the Palestinians from Lebanon. It would also deal a blow to the Muslim militias who threatened Christian domination and, after the P.L.O., were their major source of concern. Israel already had their own militia in South Lebanon, run by a cashiered Lebanese army officer, Major Saad Haddad, who would take on the role of policing the D.M.Z., a role that legally belonged to UNIFIL, the U.N. six-nation peacekeeping force which had been deployed in the south since 1978.

"Now Haig did caution—it's an interesting point—that the United States would not be able to support Israel in the Lebanon venture unless there were what he called an internationally recognized provocation. It's a very strange formulation; in the past Americans had never used the phrase with the Israelis and I think it was almost an invitation to the Israelis to either create an incident or seize upon one that somebody created and say, you see, here it is, the pretext, the provocation that we've been waiting for."— WILLIAM QUANDT

When the P.L.O. did not break the cease fire even though Israel had arbitrarily extended it to include all her borders, Begin then announced that any attack on any Israeli anywhere in the world would be the direct responsibility of the P.L.O.

"Of course this is fantastic, because no one expects Arafat to be able to control all the terrorist groups all over the world. Eventually, unfortunately, the Americans accepted even that, and General Haig in his memoirs, and even before that, admitted that, yes, any attack against a Jew or an Israeli anywhere in the world would be considered a violation of the ceasefire and would, in that sense justify an invasion into Lebanon. So it was just a question of when would the next attempt be made."—GENERAL MATTI PELED

As the spring of 1982 gave way to summer it became clear that, one way or another, Israel would invade.

"In the end the so-called provocation was a genuine terrorist action, but it wasn't carried out by the mainstream of the P.L.O. It was carried out by the deadly rivals of the Arafat wing of the P.L.O.—an assassination attempt against the Israeli Ambassador in London. The Israelis, at the time they launched the invasion of Lebanon, knew that this was an action organized by the Abu Nidal faction, not by the Arafat group, and Begin's attitude, and certainly Sharon's, was, it doesn't make any difference, Palestinians are all the same and this is the internationally recognizable provocation; 'Haig will be satisfied' is what you sense they're saying to themselves, and indeed he was."—WILLIAM QUANDT

"The Abu Nidal group were immediately arrested by the London police, so there was no question as to who did it, but as we now know from documents which were published... when our security people came to the government to brief them on who committed the attempt, Begin said, "Oh, there's no need. We don't need all these details." I mean their minds were made up.... It was immediately seized as an excuse for invading Lebanon with seven or eight armored divisions (seventy to eighty thousand men). There was no proportion between the operation launched and the incident."—GENERAL MATTI PELED

The Israeli Secret Service, Mossad, is one of the most sophisticated and devious in the developed world. After the arrest of the Abu Nidal assassins in London, it was rumored that so desperate were Begin and Sharon for their "recognizable provocation" that Mossad agents in some way acted as *agents provocateurs* aiding the Abu Nidal group with their assassination attempt.

"This was an assumption made by my good friend Sartawi, who was assassinated later on by the same group of Abu Nidal. He, in one public meeting we had together in Paris, suggested that the attempt against our Ambassador in London was so timely and met such a clear expectation by the Israeli government that he did not exclude the possibility that our Mossad somehow encouraged or allowed or accepted that this should happen. I was then asked by reporters who were present what was my reaction and I said that I'd absolutely no information regarding that. I would in this particular case accept a denial by our government without argument....I repeat, I have no information. I cannot make a judgment. I wonder why the Israeli government never denied it. The accusation is against our government, and if they feel completely innocent, they should say so. They never did say so. So as far as I'm concerned the question just remains unanswered."—GENERAL MATTI PELED

After softening up the border regions with two days of almost constant bombardment from land, sea and air, Israel invaded Lebanon on June 6, 1982.

Within a day they had reached the Litani River, within two they had gained their objective of containing an area 40 km. north of their border. The Israeli army was unstoppable. They pounded everything that moved, and many things that didn't. From the air they hit Palestinian Refugee camps and Lebanese villages alike and had the audacity to announce that the operation had been code named "Peace for Galilee."

"The destruction that resulted from that war was unimaginable, it was so huge. The terror it inflicted, the pain it inflicted on people, the blanket bombing excluded no place. Everything was exposed to bombing: hospitals, schools, farms, bridges, roads, villages, towns, refugee camps...it was indiscriminate, no one was safe because they hit Lebanese villages as well as Palestinian refugee camps. I remember the air force was bombing for 24 hours at one time, and I could see people at the verge of nervous breakdown because of the roaring of the planes and the explosions all around them, and sometimes you think that no one would survive such bombing and it was not only from the air, it was from the air, land and sea."—SALAH TAMA'ARI

Two days after the invasion had begun Israeli armored divisions were scything through the narrow coastal strip towards Beirut while others swung east, covered by the air force, which began to demolish Syrian positions in the Bek'ka Valley, the thin fertile plain that lies to the east of the mountains which surround Beirut. This sudden change of direction was, for the Americans at least, unexpected.[5]

"Sharon had a different war-plan in mind. He wanted to settle accounts with the Syrians, which nobody had mentioned to the Americans. Haig began to get nervous when he saw that there was a prospect of a Syrian/Israeli confrontation because that raises the prospect of a U.S./Soviet confrontation."—WILLIAM QUANDT

Israeli fighter-bombers smashed the Syrian positions in the Bek'ka. They destroyed their Soviet-supplied ground to air defense system, which was positioned on the road between Beirut and Damascus, and they brought down 80 Syrian planes.[6] The situation was becoming serious—there was suddenly a real danger of super power confrontation.

> "Now it is widely said but not true that the Soviets did nothing during the war in Lebanon, they stood by and let the P.L.O. and the Syrians get beat up by the Israelis. I think it's more accurate to say that the Soviets said to themselves and to the Arabs that they couldn't do anything to save the P.L.O. Nor was that their primary interest in the Middle East at that time, but they were determined not to let the Israelis topple the regime of Hafaz al Assad in Damascus and they made that clear to the Americans, they...went to great lengths to show to the Americans and to the Israelis that they were prepared to intervene in some fashion in the conflict. So, you may recall that President Reagan was in Europe trying to make one of his triumphal tours—his debut as a world statesman—when all this was happening. Brezhnev sent him two very tough messages which Reagan simply transmitted to the Israelis and said, "You've got to stop the movement against the Syrian forces," and Haig tried to argue with him not to stop the Israelis, to let them finish the job. He felt that once they'd started it, they ought to go all the way, but Reagan didn't support him. Reagan went back to the Israelis and said, "No. What you do to the P.L.O. is one thing, what you do against the Syrians has implications for the U.S./Soviet relationship." So by the end of the second week of the fighting there was a de facto Israeli-Syrian ceasefire. They didn't try to do anything subsequently to limit the fighting against the P.L.O. but the Americans had a different attitude when it came to Syria—not out of love for Hafaz al Assad but because of the super power dimension."— WILLIAM QUANDT

On June 11 the ceasefire with the Syrians was in place and Israeli armor, which had been crashing almost unopposed towards Beirut, closed in on the city. Sharon and his armored divisions linked up with his Christian allies at Baabda in East Beirut where the Presidential Palace is situated—the center of Christian power and the seat of Lebanese government.

Other divisions held the coastal roads leading south and sealed the southern suburbs. By the night of June 13th Muslim West Beirut was completely surrounded. Trapped between the Christians, the Israelis and the sea were the P.L.O. and over half a million Palestinians and Lebanese civilians. As with virtually all conflicts since World War II, super-power politics mattered little now to the trapped civilians. The 70-day siege of Beirut had began.

Israel's conduct during the siege must remain a bloody wound on the national conscience for generations to come. The nation that had been born out of the most inhuman oppression in history became the oppressors.

The fury with which they hit the besieged population knew no bounds; the bombardment was merciless. They rained shells and bombs upon the helpless west Beirutis and, it appears, with U.S. approval utilized the situation to test various new weapons. "Smart" bombs, things which home in by radar and sophisticated electronics on a specific target, were reported to have demolished a number of buildings in the "Turkey Shoot" hunt for Arafat;[7] they never even got close to the man himself, but did kill innumerable ordinary people. Phosphorus bombs and shells which cause a fire ball that burns at over 200 degrees centigrade fell randomly on the city. Cluster bombs and other diabolic so-called anti-personnel weapons were dropped in such a profusion that many of Israel's own troops were injured, as well, of course, as thousands of Palestinians and Lebanese.[8] Hospitals were targeted and rendered useless by continual shelling; the electricity and water supplies were cut off and it is believed that a new vacuum bomb which implodes rather than explodes demolished a number of residential apartment blocks killing hundreds at a time.[9]

Over the next two months, until September when Israeli forces finally entered the city, 30,000 civilians were critically wounded and over 19,000 were killed.[10]

"The Israeli invasion, if you remember, started in the first week of June. During June we were not hit—during the middle of July we received several minor hits, minor compared to what happened later on. But then throughout the days of August in which the war continued, we were shelled, I'd have to say deliberately, on a daily basis, using huge shells—we suspect that some of them were phosphorus shells that did not burn. All of them were 155 mm. shells. By August 12th, the day of the ceasefire, we had to finally evacuate our final patients, and when they left us the only thing that was left in the hospital that was usable was the emergency room, and that was just because of its location (in the basement). By that time everything had been destroyed; the wards, all of them, all the operating rooms, the kitchens, the labs, every service area inside the hospital.

I don't believe at any point was the shelling random. There was one day in particular, and that was August 4th, and I remember that very clearly because that was the day, the first day, in which the Israelis attempted to enter the city and every place in Beirut was shelled. That day 17 hospitals were shelled and it's very difficult for one to say that 17 hospitals being shelled was just a matter of pure luck, or pure coincidence. It was not. Several of our employees used to, at the end of a ceasefire, travel to their villages in the south and they would cross Israeli barricades, they would carry papers identifying themselves as employees of this particular hospital, and the remarks that they had were such that, "Oh, we hit your hospital pretty well, didn't we?"—DR. AMAL SHAMA'A, Barbir Hospital, Beirut

Within the first few days of the invasion they also bombed the refugee camps in south Lebanon, which were home for some 60,000 Palestinians. Ain Hilweh camp at Sidon was "bombed for days after the fighting stopped" until all of its inhabitants had fled or were dead, and when it was completely empty it was razed to the ground by bulldozers."

They rounded up tens of thousands of Lebanese and Palestinians in the south and shipped them to hastily created interrogation and detention centers. But it was near a small village in south Lebanon that their immorality sunk lower than anyone could have foreseen.

Just outside the quiet village of Ansar a prison camp erupted like a cancer. Built to a design which in all but the gas chambers and crematoria followed the Nazi death camp at Auschwitz Berkenau, Ansar camp brought the Israelis closer to imitating their oppressors than anything before or since.

"High towers, watchtowers, wires, tents, human beings gathered, thousands of them, in a very, very narrow place, no rights whatsoever except for the right of breathing and they should be thankful to their jailer if he inflicts less pain on them. No rights whatsoever. No law was applied in Ansar, not even an Israeli law. Not even an Israeli lawyer was allowed in Ansar."— SALAH TAMA'ARI, Head of Prisoners Liaison Committee, Ansar

"Ansar is a concentration camp. I know that I am using a very harsh word, and I'm doing it deliberately. I think it is a concentration camp. I think it is a scar on the face of the Israeli people. I think the treatment of the Palestinian prisoners there is shame that I think we are not going to erase from our collective memory for a very, very long time."—CHAIM BARUM, Israeli Journalist

"You know that a soldier committed suicide in Ansar—an Israeli soldier committed suicide! He could not bear it. He could not bear serving in Ansar Prison Camp. I remember once, a soldier was guarding, he was on duty in a section called 'The Hole.' The Hole is the interrogation section. And there were a few detainees waiting for their turn for interrogation, they were in handcuffs and shackles and with eye-cloth on their eyes, and that soldier tore up a corrugated box and offered it to them to sit on. At that, one of the detainees told him, 'You are a good person. You are a good Jew.' He looked around to see that nobody was watching, and said, 'I hate this place. It reminds me of the place where my family perished.' Of course, he meant Auschwitz. Now I don't want to draw a comparison between Auschwitz and Ansar because Auschwitz was an extermination camp, Ansar was a concentration camp, but those were the words, the very words, of the Israeli soldier who drew a comparison, and who saw a similarity even in the shape of both camps—then there is something in common, although Ansar was not an extermination camp, it was a concentration camp."—SALAH TAMA'ARI

"I don't want to be too simplistic about it. Because Germany for me means gas chambers and the stories from Ansar don't remind me of Germany to this extent. But they remind me of Germany before the actual annihilation started. Therefore I feel the bells toll to warn us that something like this might happen unless we put a stop to it. I'm not saying, and I think it would be simplistic and wrong to say, that Ansar is a death camp in the sense of Auschwitz. But I don't think that we, as Jewish people, or the Israelis are immune against racism or against Fascism. And if we don't sound the bell of warning now it would be too late later. So it is ridiculous to make senseless analogies but it is wise to anticipate the day when such analogies will be true."—CHAIM BARUM

"One thing that I, that really shocked me, something I could never imagine any Jew would do, was stamping people on their forearms or foreheads or backs for identification. Not a number. It was the IDF stamp, and you could see hundreds and sometimes thousands of people with such a stamp, with their sleeves rolled up. It happened to Palestinians and Lebanese. I could never imagine a Jew would be able to do that. Well, a stamp is not a tattoo, it's not a number, but the first thing you think of when you see the stamp on a human body you think of the tattoo. It was not done to one or two or ten, it was done to thousands of people. That I thought was shocking. Something else that was frightening is the ability of the Israeli to inflict pain without hesitation and without regret....They were dealing with an enemy who was de-humanized and demonized at the same time, and when I say the enemy, I don't mean the P.L.O. fighter or the Lebanese fighter. They inflicted pain on everybody, it was like it was not human beings they were torturing, mistreating...not human beings."—SALAH TAMA'ARI

"I think in general that the P.L.O. is an army. It's not a friendly army. It's our enemy. Now I don't see them as different than any other army in the world. Therefore they don't have to be treated like terrorists and even terrorists don't have to be treated like animals.

"I think people like Mr. Sharon and Brigadier General Eytan will be...brought to justice by the Israeli people for the war crime they perpetrated in Lebanon; the actual war was a war crime. Some of the acts against the civilian populations, the use of bombs, massive killing of people, the treatment of prisoners in El Ansar, I think the whole war was a war crime and I think these people are responsible for it, and one day they will have to pay for it."—CHAIM BARUM

As the internment operation progressed in the south, Beirut was still under siege. The P.L.O. under Arafat's leadership withdrew from the camps in an attempt to draw the shelling away from the civilians. But nowhere was it safe in West Beirut.

"I arrived to the main street [Hamra Street] and there's a garden…and the Israelis were at the sea…and they shoot a big bombing in the garden…and there's an iron door and the shrapnels come through the door, and I feel myself, I fly at the air, I don't know how much, and bump to the ground. And I didn't feel in the side of my body, nor in the hand and in the face…and I can't move my leg. And there's nobody, it's six o'clock in the morning. I began to say, 'Help me, help me.'…Nobody, because they are inside. And I didn't see because a black dust in my face, and I feel something hot come from my head. I put my hand here and I feel that I will die because my bones make…my skull was open…yes. And hot blood come out…."—AISHE, Palestinian Physiotherapist

As the Israelis tightened their grip on the beleaguered city, the U.S. Special Envoy, Philip Habib, managed to conclude the delicate process of negotiating a ceasefire and the withdrawal of the P.L.O. fighters from the country which would be carried out under the supervision and protection of an International Peacekeeping Force made up of troops from the U.S., Italy and France. With the solemn assurance of the Israelis that they would neither attack the P.L.O. as they left nor under any circumstances actually enter West Beirut, the exodus began on August 21st, and with the departure of Yasir Arafat himself on August 30th the Palestinian Liberation Army was scattered to the Arab world.

Many Lebanese breathed a sigh of relief; now the war would end. The Israelis would go home, as would the International Peacekeeping Force. Bashir Gemayel, the Maronite Christian leader, was popularly elected president. The barricades would come down, Beirut would be united once more, Lebanon would be at peace at last. Such were the pipe dreams that had conceived the nation state in the beginning; all were doomed to fail.

The I.P.F. did leave, mysteriously ahead of schedule, leaving no one to protect the Palestinian and Lebanese Muslim civilians; and then everything began to unravel. Bashir Gemayel, president for just three weeks, was assassinated.

The following day, September 15th, as Maronites raged over the death of their leader, Israeli divisions moved into West Beirut under the code name Operation Moah Barzel—Iron Brain—surrounding the Palestinian refugee camps of Sabra and Shatilla and allowing a unit of the Christian Phalange militia to enter the camps. It was later revealed that the pretext for their entry was to flush out some two thousand P.L.O. fighters rumored still to be in there; though if this had been true, neither Israel nor the Maronites have successfully explained why they only sent a few men in to combat these supposed two thousand armed and desperate men. Of course, there were no fighters in the camps, simply war-shattered civilians.

Over the ensuing 36 hours the Phalange massacred hundreds of Palestinians and Lebanese as the Israelis looked on and, by their own admission, did nothing to stop it. By the morning of September 18th as many as 3,000 men, women and small children were dead, their butchered bodies piled in macabre heaps swelling and putrefying in the Mediterranean sun.

*   *   *

"They got us together, 135 men. One man put two hundred and fifty Lebanese pounds on the ground and said, "I've got children..." and then they shot him. And then they opened fire on all of us. As soon as they opened fire I threw myself to the ground. I was hit in the legs."—Survivor (name withheld)

Lebanon

"I and a relative came to see the bodies, to find out what had happened to them. It was Sunday; we couldn't recognize anybody. We laid them all out on the ground and I, I covered my mouth and began to search. It was stinking! You couldn't tell one from another. I had bought two of my girls the same dress; one of them was wearing the dress but you couldn't tell which one. They were unrecognizable—burned. There was nothing. We put everything onto a blanket. Pieces of scalp, a hand, an ear—it was like meat."—AHMED JABER

"I'll tell you, they took a boy, just a little boy and they tore him in half. They literally tore him in half by the legs. And we screamed, 'why?' They said he would only grow up to be a terrorist! My grandson, what did he do to get killed? First of all they killed his mother—they hadn't seen him, he was asleep in his cot. He started to cry, of course he did, he wanted his mother. They took him and they killed him."—MOHAMED SAID WIHIBEH

The international outcry resulting from the news of the massacre forced the Israeli government to set up a commission of inquiry headed by Yitzhak Kahan, President of Israel's Supreme Court, with the express mandate "to investigate all the facts and factors connected with the atrocity."

Possibly the most important conclusion of the report was:

"…we assert that the atrocities in the refugee camps were perpetrated by members of the Phalangists, and that *absolutely no direct responsibility devolves upon Israel or upon those who acted in its behalf.* At the same time, it is clear from what we have said above that the decision on entry of the Phalangists into the refugee camps was taken without consideration of the danger—which the makers and executors of the decision were obligated to forsee as probable—that the Phalangists would commit massacres and pogroms against the inhabitants of the camps, and without any examination of the means for preventing this danger. Similarly, it is clear from the course of events that when the reports began to arrive about the actions of the Phalangists in the camps, no proper heed was taken of these reports, the correct conclusions were not drawn from them, *and no energetic and immediate actions were taken to restrain the Phalangists* and put a stop to their actions. *This both reflects and exhausts Israel's indirect responsibility….*"[12] (emphasis added).

"I don't think that Sabra and Shatilla was an unexpected event. In fact, I personally predicted it some three weeks before it happened. I don't think it was too difficult to predict it because, since after the demolition of most of the houses of the Palestinians they still stayed and they refused to go, it was clear that some rougher means would have to be employed to persuade them to move, and from various statements made by our Chief of Staff and some politicians regarding the situation in the refugee camps, I think it was quite easy to imagine that something like the Sabra and Shatilla affair would take place. Perhaps technically or from a strictly legal point of view the Israeli government bears no more responsibility than what the Kahan Committee defined as 'indirect responsibility.' I personally tend to believe that our government was directly responsible, but whether it was direct or indirect it was certainly predictable, and as far as the Phalangists are concerned it was only natural for them to do that since they have become very disappointed by seeing that, after all the demolition we have caused, the Palestinians were still there, which worried them a great deal. The situation was that the P.L.O. was forced to leave the area, to leave Beirut altogether.

"The International Peacekeeping Force, whose responsibility it was to look after the well being, the safety of the Palestinian refugees, the civilian population, left for reasons which were never explained much earlier than they were supposed to. Israel, who signed an international agreement undertaking not to move into Beirut, in violation of that agreement moved into Beirut, took control of the refugee camps in and around the Beirut area and then allowed the Phalangists to come in and commit the massacre. Also, it is a very special situation, I mean without parallel, and to try and explain off what happened in Sabra and Shatilla the way the government did by just not knowing what happened and so on, this is too unconvincing. And since the Kahan Commission did a very lousy job on defining exactly the responsibility of the Israeli government, I certainly feel that we bear responsibility for what happened and this falls in line with our commitment to the Phalangists to help them in every way possible to get rid of the Palestinian population."—MATTI PELED (Gen. Retd. I.D.F.), Professor of Arab Literature, Tel Aviv University

The Israeli invasion upset the precarious relationship that existed not just between Christians and Muslims but—just as importantly, as it transpired— between the various Muslim militias.

With the departure of the P.L.O. there was no longer one single dominant Muslim force who could maintain stability, law and order. Rather, there are now a number of contenders. Shi'ites and Sunni's, Druze and Communists.

"When the Palestinians were in control of West Beirut there was total security, there was no robberies, there was no murders of any kind, people went about their businesses, you know, normally. Then you had the period after the Israeli invasion, when all kinds of militias emerged on the surface and they started controlling. They were already rivals between themselves and each one of them fought the other for control of a certain area. At any one point there was a dominant force. For instance, during the Palestinian period the Palestinians dominated but they had local allies like the P.S.P., which is the Progressive Socialist Party, like the Shi'ite militia of Amal, like the Communist Party, like all other allies, you see. But it dominated, the Palestinian dominated, you see. Now after the Palestinians were gone those allies emerged and they emerged on almost equal level. Now the people who are dominating West Beirut or are supposed to be controlling West Beirut are the Druses of Minister Walid Jumblatt and the Shi'ites of Minister Nabi Berri."—TEWFIK MISHLAWI, Lebanese Journalist

Although Israel effectively retreated in 1985, retaining a token force in the south, the fragmentation of Lebanese society was total. Whether they had actually intended to "Balkanize" Lebanon or not, is now irrelevant. Confessional groups have broken down into sub-groups, and though since the first peace plan of 1984 there have been numerous attempts by the politicians to end the situation, fighting erupts constantly as each faction gains another city block or another private score is settled.

"We're talking about a completely feudal system with a very modern coating on it, which means that you have strong leading groups making the poor people fight each other…and make them want to fight each other because of cultural, religious, social feelings and as long as you can move masses of

people in this way, some people get their schemes to succeed. How can you patch this society up again? Lots of people want to live, co-exist, but now they are beginning to be pushed into hating more than they ever thought they would and they didn't mean to, initially. At least I believe them when they explain this to me—but at the next moment they'll kill!"—TRINE GRØNN, Norwegian Physiotherapist, Shatilla Camp

Whatever the sectarian nature of the civil war may have been in 1975 it has degenerated, if that is indeed possible for any war, into something that is nothing less than a gang war. Lebanon, and especially Beirut, once the Paris of the Middle East, is held in the grip of ruthless fanatics who are slowly destroying everything. Since the beginning of the war in 1975 there have been at least 320 ceasefire agreements. Not one has been successful.

"An attempt to launch a peace movement last May failed because the gunmen wouldn't let it happen. But what do we have other than hope, you know. Nine years of destruction and death, many people have left the country, those who could afford it. Many others were killed or wounded. And those who remain simply hope that the situation will improve. It is very difficult to see Lebanon going back to the way it was before the war. I personally don't think it will. But my personal guess is that the majority of Muslims and Christians in the country, the non-fighters, those who are not fighting, would very much like to see the war come to a very early end. I mean we had so much of it that physically people are unable to take any more. I used to resist all the shelling and the fighting and this and that at the beginning of the war, but now I feel physically unable to take anymore. The minute I hear a shell dropping I simply collapse."—TEWFIK MISHLAWI

"I think one of the main reasons that…that there's so much despair and so much hopelessness and there is so much negativism even among people who feel committed to a cause, whatever the cause is, it's the fact that this bodily injury keeps on coming home every day and it is so much closer, and it is so senseless. I mean, you know, if you were facing an enemy that you had established before to be your enemy, fine. But I mean who are you fighting now? Now what has happened to the country as a whole has changed matters so much that you're not—what are you resisting? I mean, who are you fighting? What are you fighting for? I mean, fighting as doctors by staying put and doing what you're supposed to do as a doctor, fighting in that sense. I mean, why are you doing that anymore? Most of the people that I talk to just ask these questions, and so many people who did not think of leaving before, or before had left only because of family considerations, are leaving now because they want to leave permanently, they don't want to have anything more to do with this country. It's a totally different way of dying. I mean you're dying not physically, but you're also dying spiritually."—DR. AMAL SHAMA'A, Barbir Hospital, West Beirut

Lebanon

"We've seen death in all it's forms. We've had enough suffering. No country in the world should have to live as we have had to.... There are 27 of us, five families living in this flat. Whenever we go out we never know whether all of us are going to get back. You never know when you go up the street if they're going to open fire. Shells can come from anywhere. The person next to you can get blown up. That is how it is. We say, if luck is on your side you'll be O.K. If it isn't—they'll get you."—Refugee (name withheld)

"The war has made a lot of problems for us. Our lives are very hard. We've always got to be on the lookout, whether our children are out in the street or at home. What can we say about the war? It's brought us nothing but pain. We want a government that can solve the country's problems, not one that will always be with one faction or another. We need an army that's non-factional, one that will protect us. We need a government that will give us our rights, not the mess we've been in. We want to live! We've sacrificed our young people, children, everything—and it's brought us nothing. Look at how we are." —Muslim refugee (name withheld)

"He was shot by sniper. It's very difficult for a boy like Tariq. And also Tariq lives a miserable life because he lose his mother, she also was shot by sniper and he live with the grandmother, with his brother and sister and he have two sisters and one brother and they live at his grandmother home. I am very, very glad when I work with people like Tariq, like I was before, because I shot by shrapnels in my head and my back and my leg, and also here—the shrapnel cut the nerve and I feel in much pain. And when I look at myself and I walk good like the other peoples, I am very, very happy. And I am very glad to help him to be a good and if I can help him, as I can very, very much, I will help him."—AISHE

"He's at the age where it's hitting him hard now. He's thirteen and this happened to him a year ago almost, and he knows what another thirteen-year-old can do. But if you look at the smaller children, it's amazing. There has been international experts coming here to see the psychological effects of the war on children in Lebanon and they don't find what they came to find, because the small children have the family structure here, as long as the mother is there, as long as the home exists the small children are really relaxed; they are happy, they are outspoken. But as soon as you leave that age group and start from six, seven and up, you see a lot of open aggression or passive resistance, meaning they pull back, they don't communicate, they don't want to talk about anything."—TRINE GRØNN, Physiotherapist, Shatilla Camp

Lebanon is divided today as never before, almost without hope of reconciliation, and the killing continues on a daily basis. Christians kill Muslims, Shi'ites kill Sunnis, everyone kills Palestinians, and so it goes on almost unnoticed.

"The whole map of the Middle East is the result of policies made far away from the Middle East by powers and politicians far from here during this century. They still have a responsibility for what's going on today...and probably our own countries are in the best position to influence the major political pressure to change it. At the same time I am pretty angry with the Lebanese now. After two years I understand their problems, I understand their anger, etc., but I can't understand that at least they can't accept their own responsibility to agree between themselves. But as a foreigner sometimes I feel we should do more and feel very ashamed because of what's the rest of the world makes of the Middle East as a playground...."— TRINE GRØNN

"Certainly Americans who think about it—and very few of them do now— would look back on the whole period of '82/'83/'84 and say why did we ever get involved in it? There was absolutely no gain. I mean tremendous illusions were entertained about the Maronites and Bashir Gemayel and strong pro-Western Lebanon and so forth. To even talk about that today you sort of wonder what people were smoking in those days that made it plausible."—WILLIAM QUANDT

When in June of 1985 the world suddenly focused its attention once more on Beirut, after a long absence from the headlines, it was to milk every drop of sensationalism out of the situation at Beirut Airport where some 32 Americans were being held hostage by Shi'ite militiamen on board a TWA Boeing 707. Eventually one of the hostages, a U.S. serviceman, was killed. President Reagan mouthed impotent threats of retaliation, though he didn't seem quite certain who he could or would hit; Mrs. Thatcher talked about the media being "the oxygen of terrorism" and the networks had a field day with live coverage of every inconsequential detail. Beirut was news again.

Less than a mile down the road from the airport is the Palestinian refugee camp of Bourg el Barajneh. As the hostage "crisis" dragged on—Israel refusing to accede to the hijackers' demands for the release of Shi'ites illegally held in Israeli jails and Reagan lacking the compassion to demand that Israel make this concession—six hundred and fifty more Palestinians were massacred by Shi'ite militiamen, but the press said virtually nothing. One dead American Marine makes much better copy than six hundred and fifty butchered Palestinians.

Every day a few more ordinary people's names are added to the list of over 85,000 Lebanese and Palestinians who have already died for nothing.[13]

"It's very difficult for me to allow anybody to die. I mean everybody's dying, I have people working over people who've come in dead, you know, and they'll give them another chance, but they're dead. There's been just so much. I mean every person is so valuable, you learn that—at least I've learned that every single person is valuable to somebody else. I mean he's totally irreplaceable and there's no way in which you can just put him down just as another casualty, as another number. And it's distressing because there's no end to this. You can't keep on hurting families and groups and individuals…with no purpose and no end, when you know that it can be stopped. I know in '82 that the war did not have to take place, that starting from day one it could have been stopped. There's a great moral responsibility on everybody who was involved at that time for it to have gone on so long. I have to impose the same kind of responsibility on people here—every man carrying a gun has a choice either to fire or not to fire. I mean, the final choice rests with him. And he has to bear the responsibility."

"As we've been talking, for the past few minutes, there's been automatic fire going on all around us…and none of us seem to react to it."

"I know, well…it's part of the background of living in Beirut!"—DR. AMAL SHAMA'A

ERITREA

"If you want to kill the fish, you have to dry the sea"

"I think that the Soviet Union wants to play the same kind of game that the United States has played in the post-war world, and of course you start with the minimum reality that nuclear war would be a mutual disaster. So all of policy has to be geared toward pursuing one's foreign policy goals without raising that risk too high. So that naturally suggests that the only arenas of safe conflict are those in the Third World where the stakes are not that high that the outcome is going to produce a nuclear exchange between the super powers, and I think the Soviet Union thought they could win just by the flow of history. The flow of history was against the colonial system, they didn't have any vested interests economically or ideologically in the existing arrangements; but now they've begun, in this second phase of post-war history, to pick up their own vested interests in the Third World, their own regimes that are confronted by nationalist movements, and I think the Afghanistan and Ethiopian situations are ones where I think they're basically defending regimes that are themselves very much opposed by nationalist movements."—PROFESSOR RICHARD FALK, Princeton University

Behind the headlines of famine and death in Ethiopia lies the almost untold story of Africa's longest on-going war. Since 1962 when the Emperor Haile Selassie, in contempt of a United Nations resolution, illegally annexed Eritrea, the Eritrean people have been fighting to regain their independence.

"Eritrea itself is not very well known outside. It's difficult for journalists to get in here and it could take three to four weeks to do an adequate job. There are considerable hardships for the journalists who come—from the lice that one has to put up with, to a lack of food and hard rocks to sleep on—and most journalists simply won't put up with it. There was a parade of journalists coming in here in 1977 when the Eritreans looked like they were about to score a victory.

"Then when the sudden turnabout came in 1978 with the massive Soviet build-up, and the Ethiopian offensive with 120,000 troops involved in a war on a dozen different fronts—the International Community simply wrote the war off as one that would never be won. There was an Ethiopian superiority in numbers and material, and based on that very superficial reading of the situation the Eritrean issue became a dead one. But the war continued after that on an enormous scale, with fifteen, twenty thousand troops sometimes killed in a week of battles. But I think another reason perhaps that's important is that Africans killing Africans is not a story.

"There are events of profound importance taking place in Eritrea, not only in terms of the impact directly on the Eritreans and the Ethiopians who are fighting, but in regional and global terms. But they don't fit the classic mould of East versus West. How do you place a left-wing guerrilla movement fighting for social changes among its people, but against the Soviet Union, and against a Soviet-backed government? It doesn't fit the conventional wisdom. Our media are so used to being able to reduce a situation to simple black and white that when it's a bit more complex than that it's put in a closet, it's left on a shelf."—DAN CONNELL, Grass Roots International

Eritrea is the name given by the Italians to the rugged land that stretches northward to Sudan from Ethiopia, which they colonized in 1890. Before the Italians and the Berlin conference of 1884, in which the European colonial powers carved up the African continent with arbitrary territorial boundries that served their vested interests, not those of the peoples of the continent—boundaries incidentally which persist today—the land they called Eritrea was never a cohesive unit. This was due in part to the varied nationality of its peoples and the extraordinary geography of the region which climbs west from a thousand kilometers of the Red Sea desert plain inland to the fertile central highlands and on to the Barka desert which borders Sudan. To the north the terrain changes again with inhospitable arid highlands cleaved by deep valleys through which seasonal rivers periodically torrent. The nine nationalities living in the region ranged from nomads, semi-nomads, peasant farmers and merchants, the more sedentary peoples living within what modern Eritreans claim were separate kingdoms and principalities. Certainly from the seventh century onwards they neither owed allegiance to nor were occupied by any imperial or colonial power, and since historically there was no unity between these nine groups it's hard to imagine that the area could ever have been, as Ethiopia claims, one of her colonies throughout her three to four thousand year history.

Even the Italians begrudgingly accepted the distinction between the two territories, leaving Ethiopia independent until 1935 when Mussolini invaded from bases in Eritrea, capturing the whole Ethiopian empire.

The fifty-year process of Italian colonization introduced a certain level of development in Eritrea; roads and railways were built creating an infrastructure superior to Ethiopia's linking the towns, where Italian-owned factories ran on cheap Eritrean labor, to the coastal ports. It also forced the nine Eritrean nationalities to recognize that they now lived within a specified set of boundaries, and in turn these, combined with all the usual immoralities of colonial exploitation, instilled within many a sense of unity and a belief in nationhood that, by the end of World War II (during which the British had captured both Eritrea and Ethiopia), would not die. But the growing economic and strategic rivalry between the super powers would ensure that nationhood was not to be.

Instead of independence—which is what they expected after 1945, or at the very least trusteeship under U.N. supervision, which was also proposed—the country was federated in 1952 into the Ethiopian empire of Haile Selassie under the terms and safeguards of a U.N. resolution, safeguards which the U.N. subsequently neither could nor would uphold.

"Ethiopia is a strategically located bridge between Africa and the Middle East and that's where Eritrea comes in. Eritrea is really the southern flank of the Middle East as well as being the outer edge of what we now see as Ethiopia. Control of Eritrea by Ethiopia gives Ethiopia access to the Red Sea and it also gives an advantage to any other country that controls, or has a relationship with, Ethiopia.... It was, in fact, the U.S. pressure at the United Nations that caused Eritrea to be federated with Ethiopia in the first place instead of getting its independence. Through the 1950s the U.S. army trained the Ethiopian army in exchange for military bases in Eritrea.... [There was] a military base in the capital Asmara with five thousand Americans working a communications installation that covered the entire African continent and the Middle East."—DAN CONNELL, Grass Roots International

Over the following ten years, with direct U.S. assistance, Emperor Haile Selassie set about the complete dismantling of Eritrean industry, its economy and political autonomy. Five hundred factories were closed down and moved to Ethiopia. The Eritreans' language, Tigrinya, was banned and Amharic, that of Ethiopia, replaced it as the language which had to be used in all schools, businesses, public offices, the law, etc. Political parties and trade unions, whose right to exist was supposedly guaranteed by the federation resolution, were also banned and even legitimate criticism in the Eritrean parliament was suppressed; the critics being imprisoned and tortured. As this smothering of Eritrea progressed, strikes and public demonstrations occurred which the police and army put down mercilessly, killing hundreds of demonstrators. Finally, in late 1962, having imprisoned or killed the opposition and having filled the ruling party with puppets, Selassie pushed a motion through the Eritrean parliament which effectively voted its own dismissal and absolute annexation of Eritrea by the Ethiopian Empire in complete contravention of the U.N. Federation resolution; a resolution which the U.N. was obliged to see upheld.

"Eritreans had a perhaps naïve notion that the United Nations would intervene on their behalf, and they raised considerable protest at the U.N. starting in the late 50s and moving into the early 1960s as the war began. The U.N. is still legally responsible for the adjudication of the dispute between Eritrea and Ethiopia because they're both bound as autonomous states. However, the U.N. has never paid any attention to this issue seriously from a political perspective."—DAN CONNELL

"The U.N. is a club of states, an exclusive club of states. If Eritreans or even Ethiopians from mainland Ethiopia wanted to come in and complain to the U.N., they wouldn't have any chance. States are members of this club. It should be called the United States of the World but it's called the United Nations. It's not nations but states that are represented there, and states have their own rules of the game. It is scratch my back and I scratch your back. When questions are raised at the U.N. by Eritreans, we are told that the road to New York is through Addis Ababa. We have to go to Addis Ababa and appeal to the Organization of African Unity, which is a regional organization...which of course is dodging the question."—BEREKET SELASSIE, Professor of International Law

"What is the U.N.? It's the sum today of 159 Governments, including yours, mine. The U.N. is an instrument. It doesn't have any powers of its own to go off and say set things right when something doesn't go right in a country, whatever it is, and it is like a bicycle. I mean it only works when people get on it and start pedaling away. If they don't, it doesn't work. And so you have the situation where people are constantly clamoring for the U.N. to do something about it when the governments are not wanting to do it. I mean that is really basically the great problem. The sort of co-operation that the U.N. was based [on], at the end of the Second World War, broke down immediately after the war, when the Cold War began, and that has put a great deal of difficulty on the U.N.'s political activities. There's no point in denying it—it's a fact, but the day that the governments go back to the charter and observe it and act collectively as was the inspiration of the U.N...., then there would be no problem with the U.N."—FRANCOIS GIULIANI, U.N. Spokesman

"Ever since the early 60s the Eritrean problem has simply been in a closet as far as the international community has been concerned. But there's been a kind of conspiracy of silence on this for decades. I think part of the explanation is that in the early years, the de-colonization movement in the rest of Africa really was in the forefront of public attention and the notion of a black State annexing another colony simply didn't catch the public attention in the way that the breakdown of White European colonialism did."—DAN CONNELL

"It's been a forgotten issue. It's gone into their data file archives and nobody is caring about it. We cannot blame the U.N. as an organization...you have the big powers having the upper hand in instigating the U.N. to be concerned about the Eritrean question. The Soviet Union and the United States at the moment have their position and are playing the card of the regime in Addis Ababa; who is to win that card is still an unresolved dispute. So I think having this influence and the position of the two super powers in mind, it would be very difficult to expect any recognition from them to the Eritrean cause, which will facilitate or make things possible for the putting into the agenda of the U.N. the Eritrea case, or the conflict in the Horn of Africa."—ISAIAS AFEWORKI, Vice Secretary General, Eritrean Peoples Liberation Front [E.P.L.F.]

Inevitably as the U.N. stood back and did nothing about the annexation, suppression spawned oppression. The opposition went underground and armed itself; peaceful protest had achieved nothing, the only way out now was war.

Haile Selassie's strategy was yet another tragic example of the conformity and selfishness of the imperial mind, which never seems to learn, either from the mistakes of others or indeed its own, and appears always to bring about its own destruction. For every action there is a reaction. When people are denied their freedom and democratic rights, when they are not even permitted a political or diplomatic framework in which to voice their grievances and negotiate, when their legitimate demands are met with violence, they are left with no alternative but to retaliate with violence.

The emperor's reaction to the armed resistance of the Eritreans was to expand and escalate the war by the introduction of considerable amounts of U.S. military assistance; between 1953 and 1971 Ethiopia received up to a quarter of a billion dollars' worth of training and weaponry, with the hardware often being sent directly to the Eritrean front even though it was officially delivered to help Selassie protect Ethiopia from the external threat of Soviet-backed Somalia, with whom he was also sporadically at war in the Ogaden.[1]

It is apparently another common fact of imperial strategy that as they increase external oppression, there is a concomitant increase of internal repression deemed necessary to counter the social and political unrest which occurs at home when ordinary people react to the effects on them of an economy which is slowly being killed by a protracted war. Thus, as the war against Eritrea continued in the north, the chasm existing between the poverty of the vast majority of ordinary Ethiopians and the splendor and wealth of the feudal rulers grew too great, and in Addis Ababa, demands for radical internal change were heard from dissidents inspired by the Eritrean example.

In the final desperate attempt to hang on to power, Haile Selassie ruthlessly struck out at his opponents, but with the discovery of the 1973 famine and his explicit attempt to hide both its existence and enormity, the moral and political bankruptcy of the emperor was at last exposed and the die cast for his downfall.

"I think the famine in the early 1970s was really one of the classics in that it built up from an intense drought in the highlands of Ethiopia from 1972 onward. The early signs were all there; most of the international agencies that were involved here saw it, yet there was no public attention to it outside of Ethiopia for the simple reason that Emperor Haile Selassie demanded a cover-up of it. He refused to talk about it. And all the agencies operating here, from the United Nations through donor governments to private aid agencies, respected that and kept quiet. As a result, the aid that came in was a trickle. Meanwhile, there were people who were coming in out of the rural areas of Wallo and Tigre provinces dying by the hundreds. They were even coming to the outskirts of Addis Ababa and being forced back by the

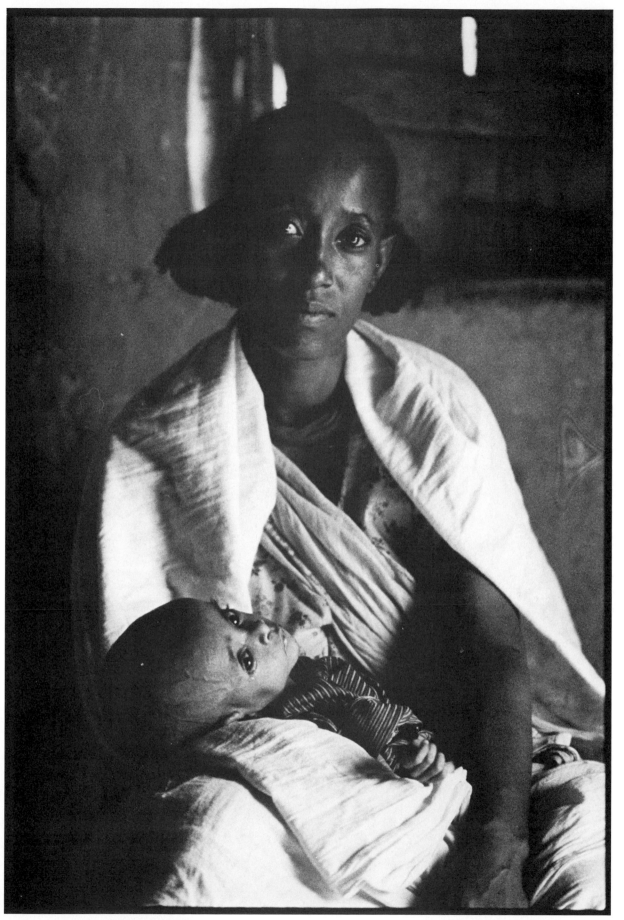

army. The Organization of African Unity had an annual conference in Ethiopia at that time, so that every government in Africa was also represented by a Head of State who was aware of the situation. Yet there was not one word in the Press outside until finally in October of '73 Jonathan Dimbleby made his classic film on the drought, and the lid came off altogether, one of the results being the fall of Haile Selassie. I would say the two factors that brought about his downfall were the Eritrean war and the famine; the famine revealing the corruption of the regime itself, its inability to take care of its own people and its unwillingness to do so. The war in Eritrea, meanwhile, tying down most of the Ethiopian army in a losing battle—and it was the army that began mutinying over this and other issues that really kicked off the process of the deposing of Haile Selassie. After that, when Haile Selassie was dethroned in September of '74, the army came out on the streets in Addis Ababa, the people came out and put flowers on the tanks, there was a serious hope in Eritrea that this could mean the end of the war. An Eritrean general was appointed head of a new ruling committee known as the Derg. But within two months he was assassinated by other members of the Derg; repression increased in Eritrea. There were piano-wire stranglings of young children in Asmara, and a deepening repression moving into an active military campaign by early 1975."—DAN CONNELL

The Derg, who espoused a certain naïve communism, were in the end no different from their old master in that they retained his grand design of an Ethiopian empire in which the strategic jewel had to be Eritrea. Rather than make peace with the Eritreans and give them what they had been asking for—a national referendum in which they would decide their future, either regional autonomy, federation or independence—the Derg elected to expand the war, in spite of the fact that the E.P.L.F. were prepared to guarantee Ethiopia's continued access to the Red Sea ports of Masawa and Assab should independence be the outcome of the referendum.

Believing that increased firepower and a larger more efficient air force could defeat the opposition, the Derg asked the U.S. for greater military assistance. But America was in the early stages of what has since become known as the "Vietnam Legacy" and they were unwilling to become further involved in another military operation which had all the hallmarks of an unwinnable war. Thus the Derg, under Colonel Mengistu Haile Mariam, turned to Moscow for help.

The Soviet Union's designs on the Horn of Africa are essentially no different from Washington's in that they perceive a relationship with Addis Ababa as having a regional political importance and access to Eritrea a strategic necessity. Neither of these perceptions are in fact valid today. Although Addis is still the home of the O.A.U. and the Economic Commission for Africa it does not have the political influence it had in the fifties and sixties over the rest of the continent, and, secondly, the strategic importance of the

Red Sea coastline has been reduced by the advent of highly sophisticated military technologies. Even so, old habits die hard and, therefore, when the Derg looked to Moscow for military assistance in 1978, the Russians were only too happy to step in and assist with the war of attrition—in exchange, of course, for the Derg's implementation of the Kremlin's form of Communism.

"One of the great ironies today is that the Soviet Union was the most outspoken supporter of Eritrean independence, arguing that all the former colonies had a right to self-determination. That position changed drastically when the Soviet Union had an interest in Ethiopia."—DAN CONNELL

"Between November 1977 and the spring of 1978, about April, not less than 1.2 billion dollars' worth of arms was transferred in one of the most extraordinary acts of intervention from the Soviet Union through Libya and Aden to Ethiopia. That was a turning point in the history of the region. I think then the Soviet decided that this was the time to go in; they went in in a big way and from that point on the Ethiopian Army had to be retrained in the use of the Soviet weapons, hence the need of bringing the Soviet advisers above all to train them in the use of those weapons and equipment. That was their mistake and I believe strategic error…they thought that they could use firepower, sheer military weight and overwhelm the Eritreans. They forgot that the Eritreans started essentially a popular war based and rooted in the people, in their consciousness, in their desire to be free, and also a war which had been by then been going for over 16, 17, 18 years with one of the most experienced leadership and also technologically capable, organized guerrilla armies I think in Africa, perhaps in the world."— BEREKET SELASSIE

"Well, for the Derg and the Soviet Union, the killing of civilians, the destruction of the economy, is immaterial. As long as it serves their policies of expansion and strengthening their position here in the Horn of Africa by making good friends with the regime in Addis Ababa, I think people dying here and being killed, the economy being destroyed, famine occurring and having catastrophic effects in the society as a whole…I think that would be very much disregarded by the Soviet Union and the Derg. That's why they're flying about 40 planes a day, around 20 sorties per day, to bombard civilians, in many parts of Eritrea."—ISAIAS AFEWORKI, Vice Secretary General, E.P.L.F.

"Beginning October there were air raids throughout the zone. October 2, Molki—a marketplace which does not have any military significance…it was bombarded. As you might have heard, 44 people were killed and 94 wounded. It was Tuesday, October 2, 1984. They very well know that it does not have any military significance, but according to their policy if you want to kill the fish, you have to dry the sea. They did it just to dry the sea, as it was there was no fish around."—HAILIE NAIZGHI, Teacher

105

Daily, Soviet-supplied Mig 23 fighter bombers raid towns and villages, often returning to the same village for weeks or months after the initial raid. They appear without warning flying low out of a shimmering horizon, screaming over the rooftops at five hundred miles an hour, their base roar terrifying the inhabitants and causing the inside of their chest cavities to shudder. At such speeds the people don't hear the planes until, at best, the last thirty seconds of the approach and therefore have hardly any chance to take cover. Those caught in the open try to claw their way into the ground in terror, for they know that if the pilots detect movement they are likely to strike again. On a good day, if they don't strike, the planes disappear as quickly as they came, leaving a fearful stillness and an echo worse than any noise their jets can make; it is the sound of terrified children.

In Decemeber 1984 they bombed and napalmed Bademeh, a small market town, killing 40 women and children. Thereafter virtually all daylight activity ceased; the market days passed in silence without people or produce and the town became little more than a dormitory as, with each sunrise, all of the inhabitants left to pass the day in the surrounding desert hiding under rocks for fear of another raid—all, that is, except Berekai Hakos, who is blind.

"During the day of the raid we were playing with the children, then the planes came. I shouted, "Take cover, take cover!" but they said, "We shall lock ourselves in our house." Then I went down into the shelter, but they were all killed—two women and three children; all of them incinerated. We cannot find our sons and our mothers. We are suffering. I am waiting until the man up there calls me.... They are fascists!"—BEREKAI HAKOS

"Many villages were razed to the ground and of course wherever possible the Ethiopian Air Force bombed civilian population engaged in peaceful productive activities. So that meant a shortage of food for many years. The present famine is not only rooted in the drought but it's also as a consequences of the...war policy of the Ethiopian Government."—BEREKET SELASSIE

"The Ethiopian government is using starvation as a political weapon, systematically to defeat the opposition movement. The international community is complicit in this by remaining silent about it because of their peculiar political interest in maintaining relations with the Ethiopian government. In that sense the Eritrean people are simply expendable, they're pawns in a larger political chess game between the West and the East. But the situation is so similar in so many ways to that of 1972 and '73. In 1973 you had an active cover up of a drought which cost the lives of a quarter million people. Today, the drought is publicized but the war is covered up and the impact of the war. The fact that over 60 percent of the drought affected people of the north, in Eritrea and in the Ethiopian provinces of Tigre and Wollo are not accessible through government channels, this has been covered up systematically by the Ethiopian government. And once again the United Nations makes no mention of this, donor governments are quiet about it and most private agencies are. The result is, I think in this case, not a quarter of a million people dying, but potentially half a million or more. So we're looking at a larger-scale problem here and yet with a common thread to that of the early '70s; the failure of the International Community...to deal with the situation as they know it to be because of political interest."—DAN CONNELL

"They're asking for relief aid from outside while they're using all their resources, the resources of the country, to crush civilian population struggling for its democratic rights in Eritrea. So I think it's a philosophy of the Soviet Union and the Derg and nothing will change that philosophy unless it's challenged by armed means and stiff resistances. The only way out to resolve the question, especially to save lives, one has to fight....As a matter of fact, I think everybody would see now that what we are paying as sacrifices, it is because we are obliged to do so that we are fighting this war. Nobody would be interested to die in any war. But since there is no other choice—we prefer a political solution but we cannot afford to give up our armed struggle...."—ISAIAS AFEWORKI

"The Soviet Union is doing things which America, you know, was doing in Vietnam. It's a source of a great deal of distress for people who regard themselves as socialists....When you talk to the Russians on an individual basis, academics and so on in conferences, they confess their own distress and they sometimes voice timidly their opposition to the Soviet support of the Ethiopian Government in Eritrea. The question is how to translate this private doubt into policy. How, how does one get the Soviet Union to realize the mistakes it's making in Eritrea? The Soviet Union decided that Ethiopia was more important; Ethiopia with Eritrea of course is more important and the hell with the rest, you know,...but it's clearly failing. You can't impose a military resolution on a political problem where the whole population is entirely against it, and able and ready and willing to sacrifice the last man and women....I wish I could be a fly in the walls in the Kremlin; you know, listen to what they're saying....There must be some questions being raised at the very least and Eritrea with Ethiopia is not Afghanistan—it's too far. They can't commit Soviet forces in Eritrea...."BEREKET SELASSIE

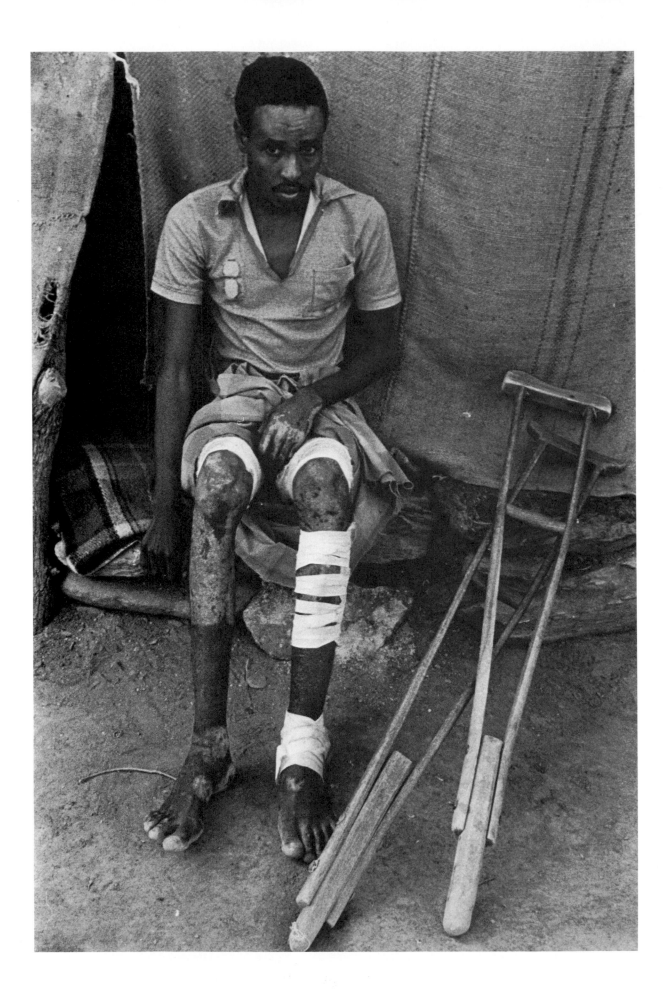

"We know we are going to die for our people and for our country and we have to protect ourselves, but these people, the civilian people, they have nothing to protect them. They are just bombing them while they are at the market, while they are in their house, while they are, while they are doing their daily business.... But the Ethiopian government indiscriminately is bombarding.... On the civilian you find napalm."

"Napalm?"

"Yes, napalm wounds."

"Ten years ago they did not have napalm. Where are they getting it from?"

"They are getting from the Soviet Union. Usually they use it through the Migs, they shell it through the Migs, especially where people are gathered."

"You mean on the civilian population?"

"Especially on the civilian population."

"Not on the fighters?"

"On the fighters also there is, but more on the civilian population...all their body burned. Some half of their bodies, some their faces, some of them are, well, you cannot even give infusion, all the body is burned. I can say more than ten years, especially this seven to eight years the Ethiopian government has used it just like any bullets or any armament, they have been using it just like anything."—Dr. Yemani Tzeggai, E.P.L.A. Field Surgeon

Napalm and its derivitive, napalm B, that glutinous obscene substance which bursts flaming from its canisters, sending out blood red globs of fire that stick to anything, particularly human beings, burrowing deep into their flesh, became almost a cliché of the nightly TV news reports when the U.S. was fighting its war in Vietnam. Could anyone ever forget Nick Ut's terrifying photograph of Kim Phuc, a young Vietnamese girl, running screaming in flames down Route 1? Sadly the answer appears to be that they could and did. For when the Vietnam war ended, napalm like the war was almost forgotten.

"This country basically has total amnesia about Vietnam. You go on the college campuses today…and the students don't even know what side of the war we fought on. You know, we get questions repeatedly, what side did you fight on, the north or the south? We've heard about napalm but what is it? What is it! You know we have to go back to these basics. You have to remember, which the American people are very quick to forget, it wasn't a police action that we fought. We fought a war!"—JOHN TERZANO, Vietnam Veterans of America Foundation

VIETNAM

"Countries don't feel pain, people do"

Vietnam's ten thousand day war of independence began in 1945 as nothing more or less than a desperate struggle to free themselves from French colonial rule. For sixty years the French were the exploiters, the Vietnamese the exploited, and like so many nations in Asia and Africa quite simply they had had enough. That their legitimate aspirations should have been so wantonly and consistently misrepresented as a Peking or Moscow inspired "communist" plot to usurp western economic and political interests, by presidents, politicians, diplomats and cold warriors masquerading as journalists, must stand as one of the greatest lies of the twentieth century. Indeed the lie should also be recognized as one of the century's greatest crimes since it led to the deaths of upwards of five million people.

It is true that Ho Chi Minh was a communist—he was a co-founder of the French Communist Party in the twenties when he lived in that country, he spent two years in Russia where he studied Marx and knew Lenin, he worked as a diplomat for Moscow in their consulate in Canton and founded the Indo-Chinese Communist Party in 1930—but, he was first and foremost a nationalist who believed in Vietnam's right to self-determination and real independence from all external powers, whatever their ideology.

Major Archimedes Patti, the first American serving officer to make contact with Ho in 1945, at which time the U.S. considered him an ally, states in his painfully honest book, *Why Viet Nam?*:

> "Whether Ho was a nationalist or a communist should not have been the issue. The fact remained that he was a nationalist first, a communist second. Ho was more concerned with Viet Nam's independence and sovereign viability than with following the interests and dictates of Moscow and Peking. With American support Ho might have adopted some form of neutrality in the East-West conflict and maintained the DRV as a neutral and durable bulwark against Chinese expansion southward. The Vietnamese had already demonstrated a fear of Chinese domination and continue to do so and have good reasons of their own for acting in a buffer capacity. Were it not for our 'communist blinders,' Ho could well have served the larger purpose of American policy in Asia."[1]

He goes on to say:

> "The apologists in our Department of State are hard-pressed to justify their supposed ignorance of Ho's nationalist character and the sincerity of his movement for independence. Their own departmental files dating from 1942 reveal that Ho and the Viet Minh were singularly nationalist and without foreign political commitments until 1950."[2]

If it is possible to have a truly non-aligned country living on good terms and at peace with its neighbors, whatever their alignment, and trading equitably within its region and the world, it could have been Ho's Vietnam:

"He believed that the (Russian) revolution had benefited the Russian people...but he did not believe that the Soviet Union could or would make any kind of real contribution to the building of what he called a new Vietnam"; equally Ho sent a message to the Americans in September 1945:

"The Vietnamese loved the Americans; they had followed its history and were looking to the United States because of the history of the [American] revolutionary war...the Vietnamese people would never fight the Americans."[3]

"He saw conclusively that China could not be counted an ally and must not, therefore, so far as was possible, be antagonized."[4] How sad that within less than a decade the United States would have forgotten this and the message that Ho had sent and be justifying its antagonism towards Ho and the Vietnamese people by "domino theories" and the desirability "in accordance with U.S. foreign policy...[for the] establishment of stable non-Communist governments in areas adjacent to Communist China."[5]

In the closing part of *Why Viet Nam?* Major Patti states quite unequivocally:

"It is an historical fact that in each of our ventures to stem the spread of Marxist ideology we became confused and consistently failed to recognize the first cause of discontent which leads subject peoples to search for a better life. Despite our good intentions, in holding that our form of democracy is the only answer, we fail to accept for other peoples the basic tenet of democracy—the right to self-determination. The inclination of American leadership is to meet the 'threat' of communism with economic and military leverage, which *in each instance has backfired.* And where we have succeeded in imposing our life style for a time, it has often proved thankless, costly and agonizing."[6] (Emphasis added.)

It's a daily tragedy for so many people in the third world that apparently the governments of the developed world on both sides have not acquired such wisdom, honesty and understanding; Major Patti could have been writing about U.S. policy towards Central America today. Or almost of Russian policy towards a number of Eastern European countries.

It's not even possible to argue that if you discard questions of morality, the actions of the developed world can be justified on the grounds that, although the third world suffers, the people of the developed world gain. They do not. No one gains in the long run, the system is "...thankless, costly and agonizing" and, I would add, quite unjustifiable and insane.

Initially Ho Chi Minh had no desire to resort to violence as a means of gaining freedom and believed that a just negotiated settlement with France was possible. Towards the end of World War II with the Japanese occupation forces in Vietnam on the brink of surrender the question of Vietnam's post-war future was in the balance. The U.S. were favoring trusteeship and eventual independence—remember this was before the advent of the Cold War and "Domino Theories"; the French wanted their colony back. Still Ho felt that there was room for a political settlement. As head of the League for Vietnamese Independence (*Viet Nam Doc Lap Dong Minh Hoi*—later simply known as the *Vietminh*) he sent the following proposal to the French government in July 1945:

> 1. That there be universal suffrage to elect a parliament for the governing of the country, that there be a French Governor-General as President until such time as independence be granted us, that he choose a cabinet or group of advisers acceptable to the parliament. Exact powers of all these officers may be discussed in the future.
>
> 2. That independence be given this country in not less than five years and not more than ten.
>
> 3. That natural resources of the country be returned to the people of the country by just payment to the present owners, and that France be granted economic concessions.
>
> 4. That all freedoms outlined by the United Nations will be granted to the Indochinese.[7]

By anyone's standards it was a just and fair offer and at the very least should have formed the basis for negotiations. The French didn't even have the courtesy to reply.

Barely two months later, after the atomic bombing of Hiroshima and Nagasaki, the Pacific war was over. The Japanese occupation forces effectively surrendered the north to the Viet Minh which had taken Hanoi, and in the south they would hand over their weapons to the British under the command of Maj. General Douglas Gracey. Gracey indeed did take the surrender in Saigon and began the process of handing the country back to the French, but within five weeks, incredibly, he rearmed the Japanese troops and turned them loose on the Viet Minh who were attacking French-held positions—General Gracey was a child of the British Empire and considered that Vietnam did not belong to the Vietnamese but to France—an act that caused General McArthur to exclaim to Edgar Snow: "If there is anything that makes my blood boil, it is to see our allies in Indochina and Java deploying Japanese troops to reconquer these little people we promised to liberate. It is the most ignoble kind of betrayal."[8]

On September 2, in the presence of Major Patti and thousands of Vietnamese, Ho Chi Minh declared The Democratic Republic of Viet Nam independent. With what would prove to be a tragic irony he declared:

> "All men are created equal. The creator has given us certain inviolable Rights; the right to Life, the right to be Free, and the right to achieve Happiness.... These immortal words are taken from the Declaration of Independence of the United States of America in 1776. In a larger sense,

this means that: All the people on earth are born equal; All the people have the right to live, to be happy, to be free...”[9]

The French were not amused; they wanted their colony and would re-take it with force. The venture was futile and murderous and would last for nine years until, with the fall of Dien Bien Phu on May 8, 1954, seventy years of colonial rule finally ended; the French war was over, the American but a few years away.

The United States, who “accepted responsibility” for the war as early as May 1950 when they began to support the French,[10] spent upwards of five hundred billion dollars, much of it on bombs and ammunition, in pursuit of an unattainable victory.

“Before it ended, five and a half million American military personnel and thousands of American civilians had served in the area: 58,000 Americans had been killed, and more than 150,000 were wounded and hospitalized. War deaths from both sides amounted to at least 1,300,000 for the period 1965-75, approximately 45 percent of which were noncombatant civilians. Almost as many deaths, most of them civilians, were said to have occurred during the period 1945-54.”—SENATOR CHARLES PERCY, Chairman: Committee on Foreign Relations[11]

Though it is shocking that 58,000 Americans died for a cause that was a lie—a lie which held that those 58,000 Americans, mostly under twenty-one years old, were defending the free world from the advance of monolithic communism which would sweep down from China—it is equally shocking that the lie is being perpetuated. In 1980 Ronald Reagan said of the Vietnam war: “Ours was a noble cause.”[12]

That “noble cause” killed not thousands, but millions of Vietnamese; at least two million five hundred thousand according to Senator Percy, whose estimate must be taken as conservative. In fact no one can be certain of the exact death toll; indeed, it is probable that the real total is nearer four million, and though the fighting may be over the war continues to claim casualties.

When, on April 30, 1975, the last U.S. Marines were evacuated so ignominiously by helicopter from the roof of their Saigon Embassy, they left behind a shattered country that remains to this day a live minefield.

A quarter of a million unexploded bombs and a staggering two and a quarter million unexploded shells still litter the rural areas.[13] Usually they are found and detonated by unsuspecting peasants working the land. As many as ten thousand have probably been killed by what the U.S. Army terms this “leftover ordnance.”

In the south of the country, in 1984, every hospital received at least one victim each week. At the Cho Ray Hospital in Cholon, Ho Chi Minh City, for example, they have had to treat over seventeen hundred since 1975 and the admissions rate is not diminishing.[14]

Mr. Nguyen was a peasant farmer. He was burning off some brush wood that concealed a discarded case of M16 ammunition. The ammunition exploded. Forty percent of his body was burned.

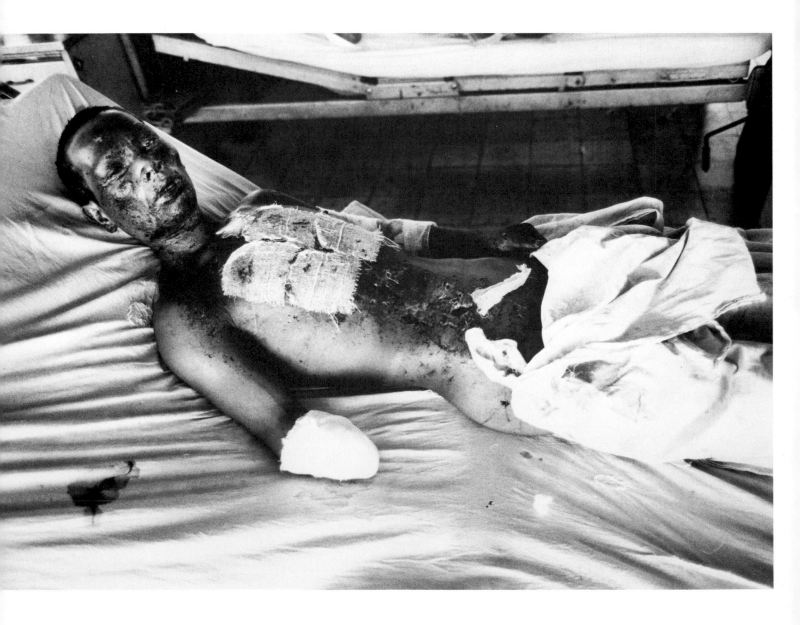

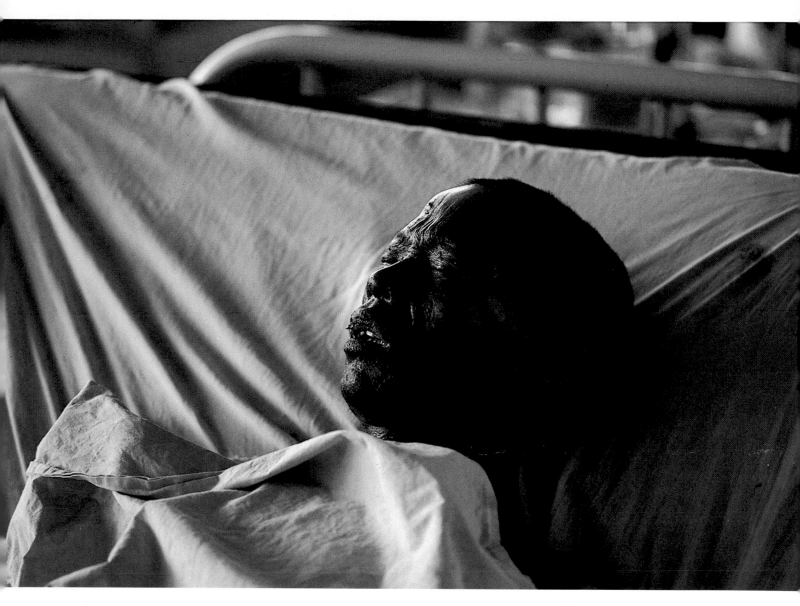

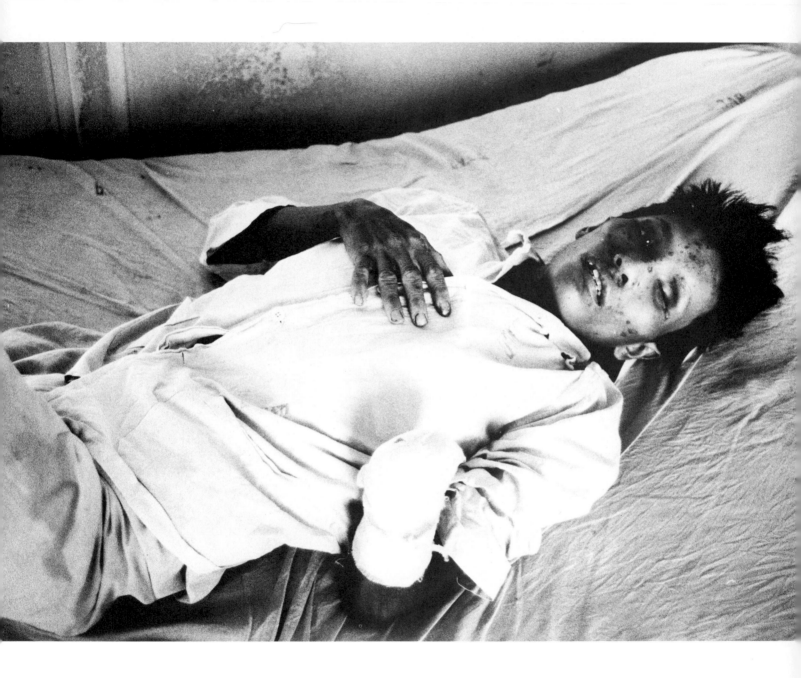

He was ploughing with his oxen. The plough turned up an M72 armor piercing light anti-tank round. The oxen were killed. He lost his left forearm and leg.

He was looking after the family's buffalo when he saw something glinting half buried in the soil. It was a 40mm grenade. He did what any boy would do—picked it up.

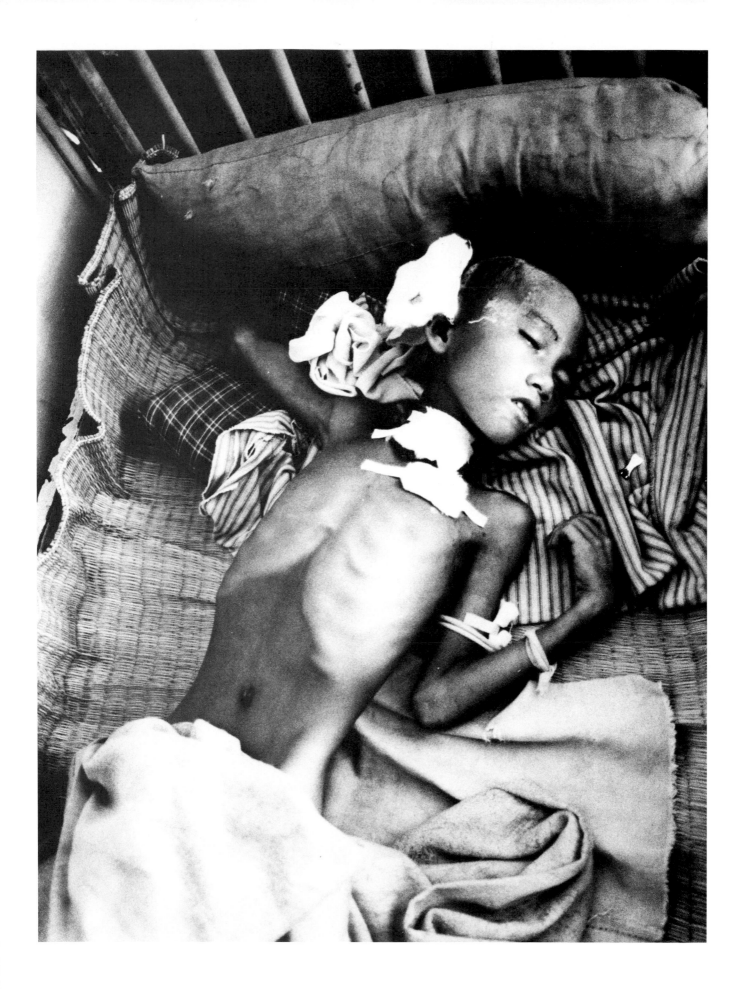

"Here is a boy, twelve years old. He was also looking after his cows and a cow has stumbled on a shell. He has a spontaneous amputation of his arm...."

"That means it was blown off?"

"Blown off, yes. The other hand, he has injuries of the fingers. His leg has multiple fractures and soft tissue injury.... He has, he feel, many pain in his right arm... blown off... and night and day. All the time."

"All the time?"

"All the time."

—Dr. Trung, Cho Ray Hospital

*   *   *

"This country has totally abdicated its responsibility for cleaning up after the war and in the ten years since the fall of Saigon, since the war officially ended this country has done nothing with, with Vietnam itself in helping them deal with the ramifications of war."—John Terzano, V.V.A.F.

KAMPUCHEA

(Cambodia)

Current Western policy which seeks most effectively to isolate and hurt Vietnam and drive her further into the Soviet camp, is part of a much larger, global power game in which the people of both Vietnam and Kampuchea are considered expendable.

The destinies of the two countries were drawn together by the French and American wars and became inextricably linked when in 1969 President Nixon and Dr. Kissinger secretly ordered the U.S. Air Force to begin carpet bombing the eastern provinces of Kampuchea, a neutral country, without informing Congress and therefore in absolute contravention of the U.S. Constitution.

Their intention, they subsequently protested, was two-fold. Firstly to devastate the Kampuchean sector of the Ho Chi Minh Trail, that most tortuous supply route of the Viet Cong (the pejorative name given by the U.S. Army to Peoples Liberation Armed Forces) that crossed into Laos from Nghe An province in the north of Vietnam near Ho's birthplace, twisted down through Laos and on into Kampuchea before fanning in tributaries back into the south of Vietnam. And secondly, to destroy a mythical N.V.A./P.L.A.F. headquarters known to the U.S. as COSVN, which they insisted was secreted somewhere in the dense Kampuchean Jungles.

On April 30, 1970, President Nixon told the American people:

"Tonight American and South Vietnamese units will attack the headquarters for the entire Communist military operation in South Vietnam. This key control center has been occupied by North Vietnamese and Viet Cong for five years in blatant violation of Cambodia's neutrality. This is not an invasion of Cambodia. The areas in which these attacks will be launched are completely occupied and controlled by North Vietnamese forces."

Brig. General Douglas Kinnard, a U.S. officer who took part in the invasion, later remembered:

"One of the things that I found interesting was…the great emphasis he placed on the COSVN headquarters, sort of portraying it as a kind of Pentagon that we would capture—and my guess is that at best it was a fox-hole and a couple of radios."[15]

This invasion, which according to Nixon was "not an invasion of Cambodia," produced 200,000 Cambodian refugees—from an area which he insisted was "completely occupied and controlled by North Vietnamese forces."[16]

The invasion had been preceded by a C.I.A.-inspired coup which ousted the Kampuchean Leader, Prince Norodom Sihanouk, and installed his ex-Prime Minister, Lon Nol, as Head of State. Sihanouk had been a master of manipulation, who managed to maintain his country's neutrality for fifteen years as he continually played off West against East and North Vietnam against the South, while at the same time placating most of his opponents at home, including the Kampuchean communists.

He was a god king who received loyalty and adulation from his people as he kept his tiny nation, about the size of England and Wales, at peace while all around war raged. This is not to suggest that Sihanouk's Cambodia was without corruption, injustice or political unrest; there had been an abortive uprising led by the few fanatical communists in 1967; however, it failed to inspire the people and factionalized the communists into smaller groups.

Lack of support for an uprising to change the status quo was in no small part due to the contentment of the majority of the population. Except for a very small percentage, in this agriculturally rich and underpopulated land, most peasants owned enough land to feed their families and make a little besides. In this and a number of other aspects Kampuchea was the antithesis of Vietnam despite the fact that both countries had been under the influence of French Colonial rule since the mid-nineteenth century. Before 1970, for example, prior to the invasion, there was no rigid class structure in the countryside, and unlike Vietnam, Kampuchea had "an almost perfect rural democracy."[17]

By ordering the secret bombing, the coup and the invasion, President Nixon and Dr. Kissinger changed all of that forever. They created famine and disease where previously none had existed. They forced thousands of peasants to become embittered refugees as U.S. war planes and artillery turned the eastern provinces into a moonscape; during six months in 1973 alone they permitted over a quarter of a million tons of bombs to be dropped.[18] Thus the expansion of America's war created the fertile ground from which a civil war would mushroom and decimate the society.

Sihanouk, now living in Peking, called upon the people to rise up and support "Les Khmers Rouges," as he christened the Maoist guerrillas, whom hitherto most of the peasants had never heard of. They were the only real nationalists, he said, fighting for Kampuchea's independence. Though it may seem strange that Sihanouk the monarchist should join forces with the communists, it was a move that suited both parties. By aligning himself with the only alternative armed force to America' man, Lon Nol, Sihanouk believed that he could regain control of his kingdom. For their part, Pol Pot and the other Khmer Rouge leaders knew that without Sihanouk as a figurehead, the peasantry would never support them.

After five years of appalling bloodshed in which five hundred thousand Kampucheans were killed and wounded, Pol Pot and his black-clad Khmer Rouge fighters took Phnom Penh at dawn on April 17, 1975. Just as suddenly and brutally as it had begun the war was over—there would be peace, at least that was what the stunned population expected. It lasted but a few short hours.

"The Americans are going to bomb Phnom Penh," announced the unsmiling young fighters. They issued orders at gunpoint that the city was to be evacuated immediately; the Angkar—the Organization—had ordered it and people were soon to discover that if the Angkar ordered it, you did it.

For once no bombs fell, but within thirty-six hours the Khmer Rouge had emptied the city of its two and a half million inhabitants, summarily killing those who couldn't or wouldn't leave. The Angkar demanded they abandon their homes, their possessions, their identities. It closed all of their borders, expelled all foreigners, desecrated pagodas, abolished religion, schools, hospitals, money, the family, twentieth-century machines and technology. Thus they embarked upon a four-year genocidal reign that would exterminate at least two million of their own people and further devastate this once beautiful land.

The Khmer Rouge leadership are mainly middle-class, Paris educated intellectuals who have little in common with the Kampuchean peasants and workers they claim to champion. Their ideology is nominally extreme Maoist but paradoxically deeply fascistic and totally impractical. Their actions and policies demonstrate as clearly as Hitler's and Stalin's did that there is no effective ideological difference between extreme political fanatics, be they of the left or right. They used the fear and resentment that the war had produced in the urban poor and the landless refugees to pit them against the bourgeoisie; anyone with an education, who worked with foreigners or the Lon Nol regime, who spoke a foreign language, became an enemy of the people and was killed. Pol Pot decreed that henceforth Kampuchea would be a peasant agrarian society and promised that it would become as great again as it had been in the tenth century when their kings at Ankor Wat ruled a Khmer Empire that stretched, he insisted, as far as the South China Sea and included eighteen provinces which today are part of the south of Vietnam. Traditional enemies were to be feared and hated, especially the Vietnamese.

Pol Pot was backed, as he is today, by China, fast becoming the World's third super power. Despite public posturings, during the war, of "fraternal friendship," China had reverted to her centuries-old animosity towards Vietnam. By backing Pol Pot the Chinese rulers believed they could accomplish a number of offensive objectives. Kampuchea would become a virtual colony—Kampuchea's only exports during Pol Pot's rule were to China; in return she got ten thousand Chinese advisers; it would be a military stepping stone towards their final goal of capturing the agriculturally rich southern part of Vietnam, and in turn this would put added indirect pressure economically and militarily on the Soviet Union; Sino-Soviet relations being at an all-time low.

The process began almost immediately. On May 1, 1975, just one day after the war in Vietnam ended, Khmer Rouge units attacked Vietnamese border villages in Tay Ninh province, massacring almost all of its inhabitants. The attack was the first of what were to become almost weekly atrocities.

By mid-1978 upwards of two hundred thousand Kampuchean refugees who had miraculously managed to escape the carnage were encamped in Tay Ninh province west of Saigon and the border raids on Vietnam continued. Fearing for their national security and having exhausted their patience, the Vietnamese invaded Kampuchea in December 1978, supported by an army of

Kampucheans recruited from the refugees. The hope was to decimate the Khmer Rouge army, remove the leadership and then withdraw, leaving a more friendly government in Phnom Penh and the refugee army to clean up the remnants of the Khmer Rouge.

The Vietnamese have been quite frank in explaining their reasons for invasion. Though liberation of the Khmer people would be the result, it was not originally their primary motive. However, as with everyone who came face to face with the aftermath of Pol Pot's Kampuchea, they discovered that knowing about it and seeing it were two very different experiences. As they swept across the country in pursuit of the Khmer Rouge, who retreated with their leaders destroying anything in their path until they reached the sanctuary of Thailand, the nightmare that the Vietnamese uncovered was beyond anything they could have anticipated, and liberation became the priority.

. Every vestige of the twentieth century had been destroyed. The towns and cities were abandoned, the jungle already reclaiming them. Two million people had been exterminated. Typhoid, cholera, anthrax and plague were rife and a further two million people, about half the remaining population, were starving to death.[19]

Suddenly the Vietnamese were stuck. There was no one to hand the country over to, except the few Kampuchean politicians who had taken refuge in Hanoi during the Pol Pot years and who would form the nucleus of a government. But there were no people to form a bureaucracy; the entire middle class had been wiped out. There was no infrastructure in place via which the famine and widespread disease could be relieved; no trucks, no cars, no fuel, no tires, no phones, electricity or pure water supplies. No hospitals, no medical equipment, or beds. No food, no drugs, no nurses or doctors—the new Minister of Transport didn't have a car, the Minister of Communications no phone—there was nothing and certainly no force capable of holding back the Khmer Rouge who had regrouped in camps along the Thai border where they were being resuscitated with western aid. If the Vietnamese withdrew, the country would not be able to continue at all; Pol Pot would come right back and the genocide would begin again. The Vietnamese had no choice but to stay.

What was recognized by people of compassion around the world as Vietnam's liberation of the Kampuchean people, was portrayed by the Chinese authorities as an appalling act of expansionist aggression against their ally Pol Pot, while the Western nations stayed silent.

Without warning but with, it would appear, tacit Western approval, 600,000 Chinese troops crossed Vietnam's northern border in February 1979 to "teach Vietnam a lesson." (Strange that no one proposed teaching Tanzania a lesson when they invaded Uganda and liberated that country from the despicable Idi Amin Dada.) Although they wrought tremendous damage, and

killed many Vietnamese, the Chinese were not as successful as they claimed. How could they hope to be? They were attackaing a people whom they had been unable to master for two thousand years, a people who had just lived through thirty years of war and had been, militarily at least, victorious over the most powerful nation on earth. Eventually, after suffering considerable casualties, the Chinese withdrew, having destroyed much of that season's rice and other crops.

From well-hidden fire-bases in the jagged hills and mountains that are the Sino-Vietnamese border they continue spasmodically to rain artillery onto Vietnamese territory.

* * *

"This is hill 600. It is the most northerly forward artillery observer position in Vietnam.... Over there, that is China. Most time we just wait.... It's O.K. They know where we are, we know where they are... they will see you as we see them. They will not fire today, today they are making work on the new road, it will mean they can bring supplies right to the border even in the rainy season."—Vietnamese soldier, Hill 600

Prior to the liberation of Kampuchea and the Chinese invasion, it seemed that Vietnam's years of isolation were really over and that post-war development and growth were going to take off. Dialogue between Vietnam and the United States had improved to the point where normalized diplomatic relations were almost a fact. Both countries had chosen sites for embassies in the respective capitals. Robert McNamara in his role as head of the World Bank had been so impressed by Vietnam's economic progress that he had recommended huge development loans.

Many western nations were opening up trade with Vietnam and humanitarian and developmental aid was beginning to flow from the E.E.C. countries. However, there were still those in Washington to whom normalization with Vietnam was anathema, they could never forgive the Vietnamese for winning their independence. Neither could they condone the fact that the Soviet Union was increasing its influence over Hanoi, albeit that, at this stage, Hanoi was managing to keep that an arms-length relationship and given the opportunity would much rather have had free trade with the U.S. But rapprochement between China and the U.S. had happened and suddenly the most populous marketplace on earth was opening up to the West. The sale of Coca-Cola, color televisions and military equipment became more important suddenly than the "fight against communism," and such was the desire not to offend the new customer and ally, what China wanted, China got. And China wanted to punish the Vietnamese for liberating the Kampuchean people from her ally Pol Pot.

The normalization process ceased immediately, with the U.S. introducing all manner of new conditions before they would consider a return to those discussions. The loans from the World Bank never materialized and supplies of E.E.C. humanitarian aid to Vietnam were stopped. Pressure from the U.S. and China in the United Nations ensured that the new government in Phnom Penh would not be recognized by that organization; western nations would continue to regard Pol Pot, proportionately the greatest mass-murderer since Hitler, as the legitimate representative of Kampuchean people.

The Chinese rearmed the Khmer Rouge as western donors ensured that excessive food supplies flowed un-monitored to them, meanwhile insisting that extraordinary conditions be met before granting desperately needed relief aid to Phnom Penh to help them claw their way out of the abyss. Allies of the U.S. were suddenly less interested in trading with Vietnam, and within a few months its isolation was complete; the "punishment" was being meted out.

Today the Vietnamese are literally trapped. They are pinned down along their wild common border with China and in Kampuchea their forces are all that stand between the people of that country and the Khmer Rouge. Such is the effect of the Pol Pot years on ordinary Khmers, they have experienced so much horror, that they appear to have lost the will to defend themselves. Even today, after seven years of extensive training by the Vietnamese, they would be incapable of any credible resistance to the Khmer Rouge. The operations on the two borders are costing millions of dollars a week but because of Western economic isolation Vietnam cannot earn enough foreign currency to pay the Soviet Union which is financing her, so the Soviet Union is thereby shortening the leash. In the meantime the U.S., China and their allies continue to demand Vietnam's complete withdrawal from Kampuchea.

The paradox is that the Vietnamese would like to retreat from both borders; remaining means continued economic and political isolation, but retreat would be death.

"Current U.S. policy towards Vietnam is punitive and petty. There is a trade embargo imposed on Vietnam. The embargo is also against Cambodia, North Korea and Cuba. It's a complete embargo on all trade of any sort. There is an exemption in law for assistance to meet emergency needs. This law goes back to 1917, the Trading with the Enemy Act, but unfortunately the only action required is that the President review annually the embargo and then reimpose it based on his perception or his statement that there's a state of emergency existing. So every year the President repeats the statement that a state of emergency exists between Vietnam and the United States and between Cambodia and the United States. The justification for the state of emergency is defined in law by Congress. There are several reasons why the Executive can declare a state of emergency: The one that applies to Vietnam and Cambodia has to do with foreign policy, i.e., that if there were not an embargo against those countries, you would have a detrimental affect on United States foreign policy. Now, any humanitarian agency that gets its funds from the American people is required by law to secure a license, essentially an exemption from the Trading with the Enemy Act. The final ruling on the license is actually made by the Department of State, since this is a foreign policy consideration. One of the reasons that the State Department gives for denying this sort of aid is that we must increase pressure on Vietnam to force Vietnam to change its policy vis-a-vis Cambodia. That would mean in extension the U.S. is attempting to force the government of Vietnam to change its policy by putting pressure on individual Vietnamese. I remember several years ago a State Department official said in Congressional testimony that the policy of the United States is to cause pain, to cause the Vietnamese to feel pain; but countries don't feel pain—people, individual people feel pain."—BILL HERROD, Church World Services

On January 13, 1962, three years before the U.S. began committing large numbers of troops to Vietnam, they embarked on "Operation Hades." On January 3rd President Kennedy had authorized the "limited operational testing" of defoliant herbicides along a sixteen-mile stretch of road west of Saigon.[20] The objective was to deny the Viet Cong food and cover by spraying and thus killing the jungle with a chemical compound known, because of the orange identification band on the storage drums, as Agent Orange. Agents White, Pink, Blue, Green and Purple were also tested, but Agent Orange, first used by the British in Malaya, was found to be the most effective.

Agent Orange is a fifty/fifty mixture of two chemicals; 2-4-D and 2-4-5-T. An unavoidable by-product of this chemical reaction is the creation of a third chemical, 2,3,7,8-TCDD. In lay language, Dioxin.

Dioxin is considered to be one of the most toxic substances known to man, one thousand times more potent than Thalidomide in its carcinogenic and teratogenic effect.

In the early sixties little was known about any of the chemicals used as defoliants, but by the middle of that decade Vietnamese peasants were beginning to manifest an alarming increase of cancers and birth defects. However, the Chemical Warfare Units, whose motto for the operation was "Only we can prevent forests," continued the spraying but under a new, more homely name, "Operation Ranch Hand." Considering the sizzling lifeless land and the human consequences of the spraying, "Hades" was not a bit too descriptive.

The first official indications that Dioxin was dangerous came from a report prepared by the Bionetic Research Laboratories which undertook a study for the U.S. National Cancer Institute between 1965 and 68. They reported teratogenic effects in test animals. But the report was simply filed and forgotten and then reappeared during the summer of 1969 in the offices of the U.S. Food and Drug Administration whereupon it was taken seriously. The Department of Agriculture instantly banned the use of Agent Orange in the U.S., where it was also being used as a herbicide.

But over in Vietnam U.S. Chemical Warfare units continued to rain Dioxin on the land and its people until the summer of 1971! Two years and many cancers later.

Just an ounce or so of Dioxin dropped in the water supply of a city like New York or London would kill its entire population. Yet by the end of the spraying in June 1971, eleven million gallons of Agent Orange containing two hundred and forty pounds of Dioxin had been dumped on Vietnam.[21]

Fifty percent of its jungles, 41 percent of the coastal mangrove forests and 40 percent of the rubber plantations were destroyed and, it is estimated, will not recover for at least forty years.[22] The human cost is even more frightening. In a country that knew few of the cancers and genetic mutations synonymous with the developed world, peasants constantly give birth to babies with deformities hitherto unknown in South East Asia. Babies without limbs, babies with no eyes, babies with no brains are now commonplace.

> "The types of birth defects that we have seen in Vietnam—the cleft palates, the hydrocephalic babies and the like—are very similar to some...seen here in the United States. There is a major difference, however, and that is the number of birth defects in Vietnam. In travelling to the orphanages and

CHEMICAL FACT SHEET*

Physical Information

CHEMICAL NAMES: 2,3,7,8-Tetrachlorodibenzo-p-dioxin; TCDD.
Dioxin, TCDBD: Cas 1746-01-6.

APPEARANCE: Colorless or white powder.

ODOUR: None.

Health Hazard Information

NOTE: 2,3,7,8-TCDD is one of the most toxic synthetic chemicals.

Inhalation: Can cause burning sensation in nose and throat, headache, dizziness, nausea, vomiting, pain in the joints, tiredness, emotional disorders, blurred vision and muscle pain. Itching, swelling and redness, followed by acne-like eruptions of the skin known as chloracne commonly occur. Symptoms of chloracne may appear weeks or months after initial exposure and may last a few months or up to 15 years. Can cause abnormalities of liver, pancreas, circulatory system and respiratory system and death.

Skin: Contact with very small amounts can cause chloracne.

Eyes: Can cause burning and irritation.

Ingestion: Can cause effects described under inhalation.

Animal studies suggest that daily exposure to amounts smaller than one grain of salt may cause severe symptoms and death within a few weeks.

Long-Term Exposure: Can cause effects described under inhalation, especially chloracne as well as numbness and tingling in arms and legs. A blood abnormality may occur which may include light-sensitive skin, blisters, dark skin coloration, excessive hair growth and dark red urine. Reproductive problems and an increased susceptibility to infection may occur.

TCDD is considered a carcinogen because extremely low levels cause cancer and birth defects in animals.

*Prepared by the Bureau of Toxic Substances Assessment, New York State, Department of Health.

some of the hospitals, not only are the numbers, it appears, significantly higher, there also appear to be some very, very serious birth defects, with some cases so horrific that it's a wonder that some of these children have even lived. We have not seen the major catastrophic birth defects here in the United States that we have seen over in Vietnam."—JOHN TERZANO, V.V.A.F.

After the war had ended, U.S. servicemen who had served in Vietnam either as part of a Chemical Warfare unit or on the ground in areas that were exposed to Agent Orange, began developing a variety of cancers and skin diseases, and were fathering children with all manner of deformities. Some two hundred and forty thousand of these men and their families decided to bring an action in the court against the manufacturers, chiefly Dow Chemical. Dow in turn brought a countersuit against the Pentagon, charging that they had not adequately instructed their troops in the safe use of the defoliant. Claims and counterclaims lumbered through the labyrinth that is the American legal process until, in 1985, a judge brought the lawyers representing both sides together. He observed that the companies had lost millions as a result of the adverse publicity the case was attracting and that the veterans might never be able to prove to the satisfaction of the court that Dioxin was the cause of their problems. He said that the case could drag on for years and therefore recommended that both sides agree to settle out of court. Finally an agreement was reached and a sum in the region of 180 million dollars was to be made over to the veterans and their families. However, one of the conditions of the settlement was that it would be publicly understood that the manufacturers were not legally acknowledging responsibility. In other words, they were covering their backs in case any other peoples contaminated by their product tried to get compensation; like the Vietnamese, for example.

During the same period the Vietnamese, isolated by the western world, were trying desperately to draw attention to the plight of thousands of their own people suffering from the effects of exposure to Dioxin.

"Unfortunately there's no trickle-down effect for the Vietnamese. It probably hurts their case for the following reason: the judge has said in his opinion Vietnam veterans would not have been able to prove their case in court. With the judge coming out and saying that and saying that in very, very strong terms, the Vietnamese, who were beyond a shadow of doubt the most heavily exposed group of people, are not going to get any sympathy not only from the American community but I think also internationally. That's been one of the things we have said all along, you know, what about the Vietnamese? What are their after-effects? The American scientific community has basically—except for a few individuals who have travelled there over the years and assisted the Vietnamese—have basically thrown up a wall between America and Vietnam. It's almost as if some people have the impression that Dioxin becomes benign the farther away it is used from the United States!"—JOHN TERZANO, V.V.A.F.

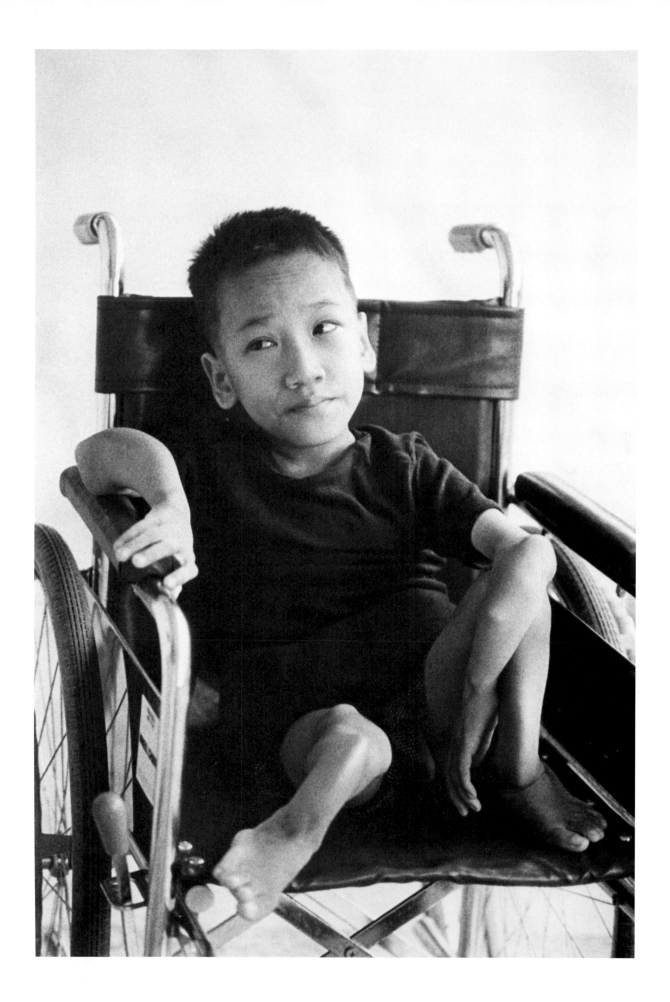

"She's nine years old. She's totally blind."

"How long was the father in the south and exposed to dioxin?"

"He was at the front from 1964 to 1973."

"And so he was sprayed...?"

"Yes. And after that he went to, to the north. Before he have two children, O.K. But with different mother, she was killed."

"So he had two normal children, but with a different woman?"

"Yes."

"Was there in the mother's family, or in his family, a history of birth defects before this child?"

"In the history of the family, the father and the mother's family there is nobody who has the defects in the family."

"Now they also have another child, yes?"

"They have another child also blind, and she die three months after birth."—DR. TON DUC LANG, Viet Duc Hospital, Hanoi

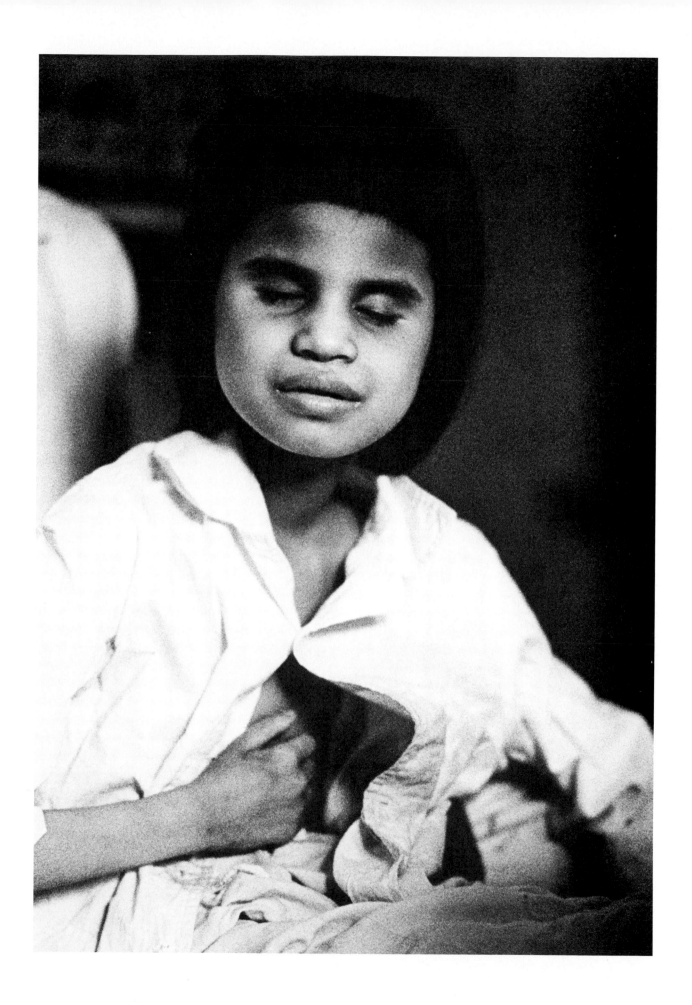

As one of the side agreements resulting from the Paris Peace Settlement of 1973 between the U.S. and Vietnam, President Nixon had promised in an eight-page letter to Phan Van Dong, three and a quarter billion dollars to help Vietnam cope with the effects of the war; the Vietnamese are still waiting for that money.[23]

As they wait, and the effects of the economic embargo bite deeper into everyday life, increasingly fewer drugs and medical equipment are available and more and more women conceive babies that are delivered still-born— grotesque aberrations of creation. Many survive after a fashion, deformed physically, mentally and sometimes both, swelling the overcrowded hospitals and children's homes while the adults slowly die of all manner of Dioxin-induced cancers.

On February 20, 1980, Mrs. Ho Thi Hue, the wife of a peasant farmer, Mr. Nguyen Thang, gave birth to twin boys. The parents already had two other healthy children born during the war when the family lived in the Mekong Delta. In 1976 they moved to Gia Lai-Kong Tum. Though their home in the Delta had mercifully been spared spraying, Gia Lai-Kong Tum had not, but Mr. Thang and his wife were unaware of this.

The twins, Viet and Duc, were healthy at birth; small, but so are many twins. They were remarkably similar, also like many twins. As they grew and their individual personalities began to form the emotional and almost telepathic bond which is peculiar to identical twins also grew. They were intelligent, boisterous, fun-loving and mischievous. They liked soccer and most other games, and though Duc would rather play than study, Viet enjoyed his schoolwork. In short, they were just like any other twin boys except for one major difference. Viet and Duc are what the medical profession calls *conjoined;* in other words they are Siamese twins.

Because of the manner in which Viet and Duc were joined it was impossible to perform a separation operation without the loss of one of them. Mr. Thang and his wife felt they were unable to cope and in truth probably didn't want to, so the babies were taken to the Viet Duc Hospital in Hanoi, after which they were named, and later to the Tu Du in Ho Chi Minh City (formerly Saigon), which became their home.

Here they ate, slept, played and began their schooling. On Sundays Dr. Sy Hung, the director of the hospital, would take them for rides out of the city, propped up in the back of his aging car. Viet and Duc adopted the medical team that have looked after them since 1982 as their family. Muoi, an extraordinarily dedicated and compassionate woman who is senior nurse, has become mother; Dr. Sy Hung is grandfather; and Dr. Diem Huong, sister. Other nurses and doctors have variously been adopted as aunts, sisters and a grandmother, and their much-loved Dr. Phuong became Aunt.

The Tu Du and its staff are constantly hard-pressed to meet the needs of their patients. President Reagan's continued prohibition of trade with Vietnam

means in practice that the country is not able to earn foreign currency and therefore cannot afford to buy adequate supplies of drugs and up-to-date medical equipment to meet the needs of a population of sixty million people suffering the legacy of thirty years of war. For example, in the developed nations it is now standard practice to give pregnant women an ultra-sound scan to ensure that the fetus is developing normally. It is possible with these machines in conjunction with certain other tests to detect genetic abnormalities very early and therefore give the parents the opportunity to terminate the pregnancy if that is what they wish. The need for such machines in Vietnam is obvious in the overburdened hospitals and in the faces of pregnant women who fear that their child might be deformed.

> "Why do they do this to us, why? Why do they want to make us suffer? There are twenty million women who can have children and we have only the one ultra-sound scan which we can take round to their villages—one. In Vietnam you know they cannot sometimes get from their village to the hospital, it is sometimes a long way, for them it is very hard and maybe sometimes even they don't think of it. So the hospital has to go to them. A German lady gave us one machine, mobile, the one we have, but only this for twenty million women.... We must have money to get more but they are very expensive, we don't have... about twenty-five thousand dollars, its so much money." DR. PHUONG, Tu Du Hospital, Ho Chi Minh City,

On May 25, 1986, Viet developed a mysterious fever and two days later lost consciousness, sinking into a coma.

After he had gone into the coma, Bacterial Encephalitis was diagnosed. This disease can be arrested before the coma stage if detected early enough, but for that, certain tests have to be carried out and the Tu Du don't have the modern facilities necessary, facilities taken for granted in the developed world.

Whether or not Viet and Duc are Siamese twins because of Dioxin is something that may never be known and is almost irrelevant now, since nothing can alter the fact that they have only two legs and one pelvis between them. But they are a symbol of Vietnamese post-war suffering. Without the Trading with the Enemy Act, Vietnam would probably have the drugs and equipment to have prevented Viet sinking into the coma.

Thirteen days into the coma, Viet is sufferring severe convulsions and is not showing response to light, sound or pain. The doctors fear he may never come out of the coma. In a profession that encourages compassion but eschews emotional involvement with patients, it is rare to see doctors and nurses weep. But there is something special about Viet and Duc. After Duc had eaten lunch at mid-day on June 9, Nurse Muoi cried quietly. Duc did not see the tears, he had just taken two pills. As he popped the first one into his mouth he said, "This one's for Viet," and then, "This for Duc."

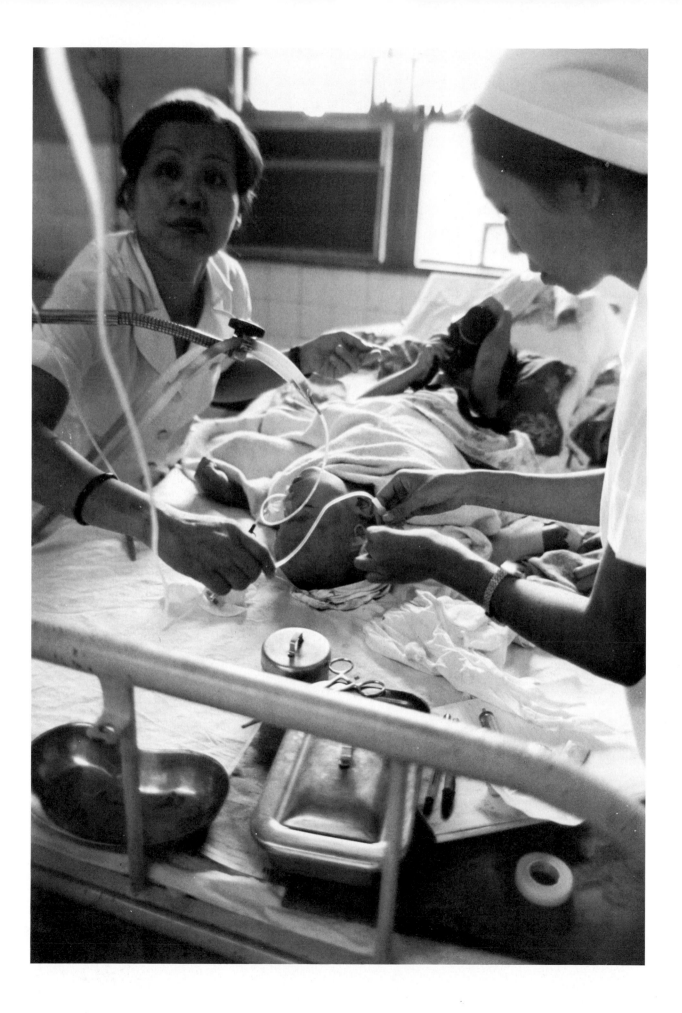

"This morning Duc ask me, 'Please help my brother and we can play again.'
He does not know—he does not understand. Even until yesterday he
thought Viet was sleeping, he is only six and does not know how serious it
is. When Viet has a convulsion now, Duc he massage Viet's leg to try to
help.... Maybe we will have to sacrifice Viet to save Duc...."

Dr. Phuong fell silent, her eyes red with tears of pity and anger.

By June 18 Duc had not been able to move for three weeks. His patience
was incredible. One day he asked for one of my cameras. This was Duc's world
as he saw it.

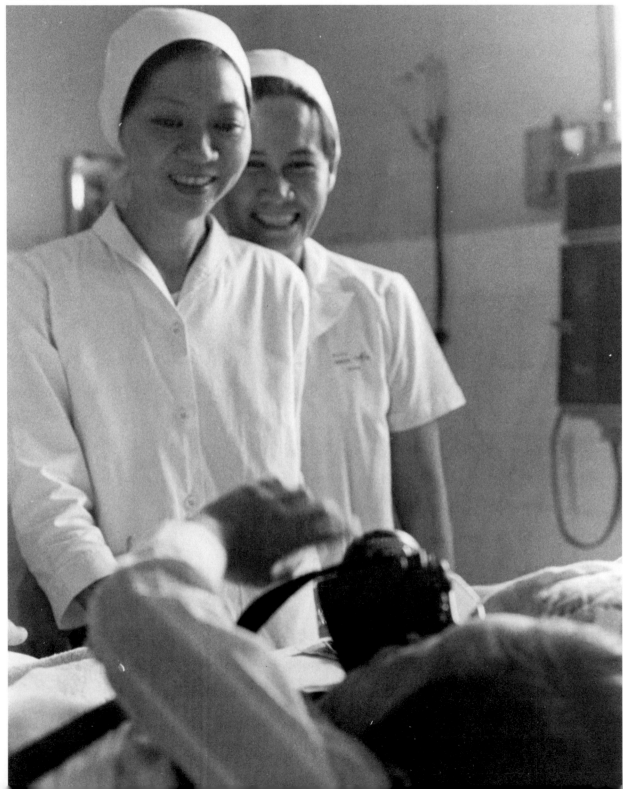

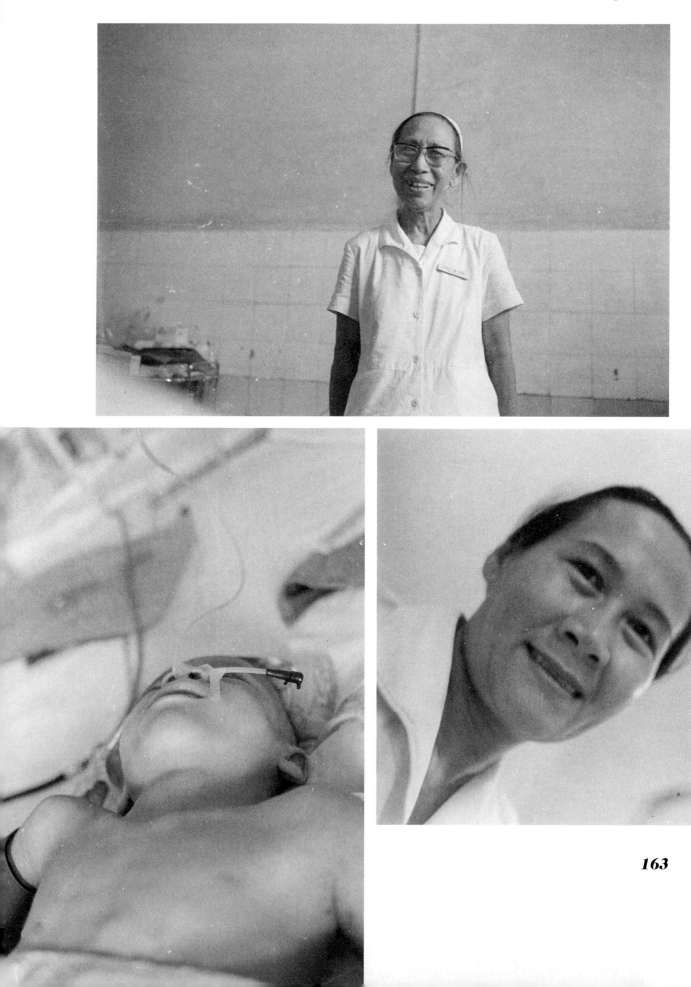

On June 19 the Japanese Red Cross responding to an appeal from Dr. Phuong flew Viet, Duc, Dr. Phuong, Nurse Muoi and Dr. Son Phat to Tokyo for the best treatment possible. However, as I write this on September 15, 1986, Viet is still in a coma in the Intensive Care Unit of the Japanese Red Cross Medical Center and Duc still doesn't understand geo-politics. He hasn't heard of the Trading with the Enemy Act or that giving medical supplies and drugs to Vietnam would endanger U.S. foreign policy. All he knows is that he has not been able to move for four months because his brother is in a coma.

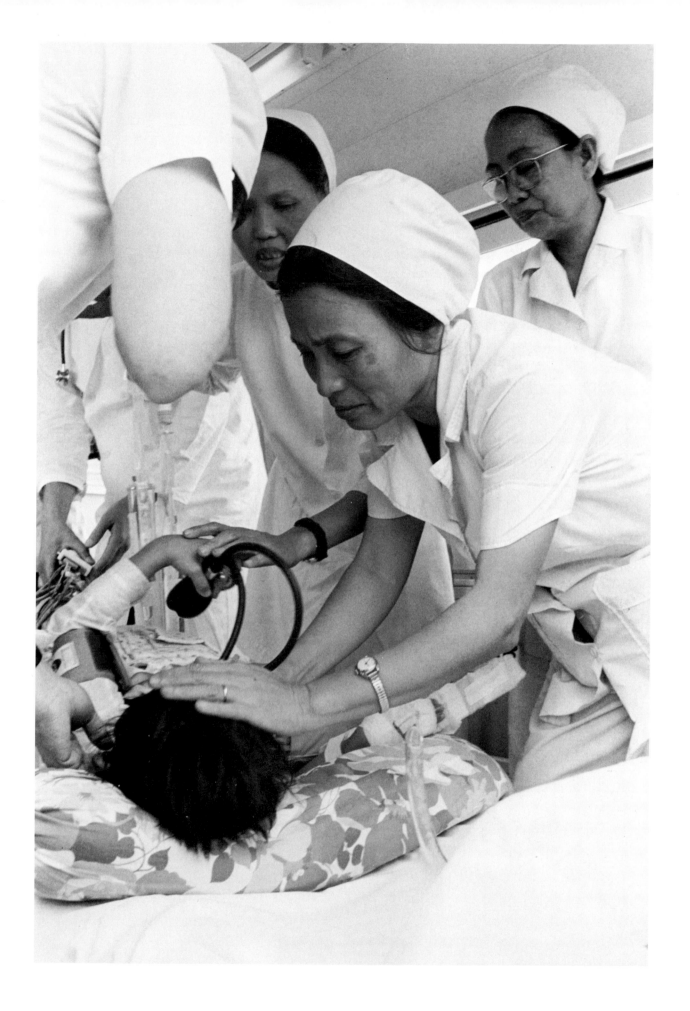

Hundreds of thousands, possibly millions, of words have been written about Vietnam, the war and its legacy. At the same time much is being done today to re-write the history in order to justify the obscenities of the past and better serve current policy. However, there remain certain unalterable truths. That the Vietnamese were given no alternative by the French but war was a tragedy.

That that war should last for thirty years because of the greed and selfishness which characterizes the Cold War of the super powers and into which Vietnam was sucked, remains a crime which can never be pardoned.

But the fact that the policy of isolation and punishment is permitted to continue is unconscionable.

If, in the sixties and early seventies, Vietnam became the watershed of strategy for de-colonization struggles and a rallying cry for radical political thought together with the nascence of a new and more compassionate approach to the rest of the world (and where, oh where is that belief and courage cowering today?); it also encouraged in the West and particularly the United States a greater belief in the "containment" dictates of people like George Kennan (quoted earlier) and an enhanced doctrine of governmental deception that persists today and whose consequences still obtain in Southeast Asia, Central America and Africa.

"We have failed, I think, as a nation to learn and understand about our involvement in Vietnam and how we got involved, and a country that isn't willing to learn by its mistakes is bound to repeat those same mistakes. And I think that's where we're heading, down in Central America. We're getting involved in a situation down there that the United States really has no business being involved in, and I feel...one of the biggest fears that we have as the last generation of American men and women that this country sent to war is just that, that we will not be the last generation this country sends to war. And I think unfortunately in our lifetime, in my lifetime, we'll be doing it again, and that I think is the saddest tragedy to come out from Vietnam—that we did not learn and we're bound to repeat it again."—JOHN TERZANO, V.V.A.F.

EL SALVADOR
"Supporting the Black Hats"

The repetition has already begun. In El Salvador U.S. military advisers, most of whom cut their teeth in Vietnam, direct the war from an embassy that stands fortress-like over San Salvador. As if in some bizarre action replay of Saigon, the air shudders to the constant chatter of helicopters and to date the U.S. government has given more than one and one half billion dollars' worth of weapons, assistance and training to the Salvadoran army.

"A well-orchestrated international campaign, designed to transform the Salvadoran crisis from the internal conflict to an increasingly internationalized confrontation, is underway. With Cuban coordination, the Soviet Bloc, Vietnam, Ethiopia and radical Arabs are furnishing at least several hundred tons of military equipment to the Salvadoran leftist insurgents.... The Communist countries are orchestrating an intensive international disinformation campaign to cover their intervention while discrediting the Salvadoran Goverment and American support for that government.... We will not remain passive in the face of this Communist challenge; a systematic, well-financed, sophisticated effort to impose a Communist regime in Central America.... We believe, in all sincerity, we have no alternative but to act to prevent forces hostile to the U.S. and the West from overthrowing a government on our doorstep...."—U.S. SECRETARY OF STATE ALEXANDER HAIG, February 17, 1981

The issue in El Salvador and indeed all of Central America is but a metaphor for first and third world relationships and is rooted principally in hunger, oppression and injustice rather than any specific ideology.

Though statistics can be, and often are, manipulated to prove any argument, El Salvador's are frightening and incontrovertible:

- 2% of the population owns 60% of the land. 8% of the population receives 50% of the national income.
- 96.3% of the rural population have twelve acres of land or less.
- In 1975, 58% of the population earned less than $10 per month.
- The per capita income is the lowest in Central America.
- The majority of the rural population has work for just one-third of the year.
- Unemployment and underemployment in rural areas is a constant 45%.
- 64% of the urban population lack sewage services.
- 45% of the population has no drinking water on a regular basis.
- 70% of children under five are malnourished.
- The per capita calorific consumption rate is the lowest in the western hemisphere.—ROBERT ARMSTRONG and JANET SHENK, N.A.C.L.A.

"I was in Salinas, California, as a family physician in about 1980 or '81 and in a volunteer farmworker clinic I began seeing refugees from El Salvador. Prior to that the issue had been largely abstract but seeing people with physical and psychological marks of torture transformed it into a very

human dimension. About that same time I was hearing echoes of what I'd heard as a young man; when I was 17 it had been: 'If we don't stop them in Vietnam, we'll have to stop them at the Golden Gate Bridge.' And I had responded to that call.

"When I was 37 it was: 'If we don't stop them in El Salvador, we'll have to stop them at the Rio Grande,' and 'them' were people I was seeing. And they were small farmers, they were priests, they were physicians like myself, who fled when the army ransacked the nation's only medical school. They were a spectre of the Salvadoran society accused of being Communists for standing up and trying to bring about some social change or for addressing issues of injustice."—Dr. CHARLIE CLEMMENTS, M.D.

Although there are few actual similarities between El Salvador and Vietnam, there are tragic echos in U.S. attitudes, policy and strategy.

SAIGON, Vietnam, November 9.

The United States Air Force has begun a huge supply and training program here to strengthen South Vietnam's defenses against intensified Communist guerrilla operations. The nature of the program was defined—within the limits of 'security'—by an official source today....

Globemaster transports have been flying into South Vietnam for the last week with equipment for bombing planes.... In addition to the bombers, fighter planes and helicopters are included in the program....—NEW YORK TIMES, Friday November 10, 1961

"The present level of U.S. military assistance to El Salvador is far too low to enable the armed forces of El Salvador to use these modern methods of counter-insurgency effectively.... The combination of the tactical guidance given by U.S. advisers and levels of aid inadequate to support that advice creates a potentially disasterous disparity between U.S. military tactics and Salvadoran military resources. U.S. tactical doctrine abjures static defense and teaches constant patrolling. But this requires the provision of expensive equipment such as helicopters."—Report of the National Bipartisan Commission on Central America, chaired by Dr. Henry Kissinger

"Well, it was in the spring of 1981 that the United States began sending advisers and helicopters to El Salvador. I saw a film about a massacre that had occurred in a rural area and an American priest described how the helicopters hovering over the Rio Sumpul had contributed to the massacre of about 600 women and children fleeing a search and destroy operation of the Salvadoran army. I knew that helicopter was non-lethal military aid. I understood the language of intervention. President Carter had sent those helicopters there as non-lethal military aid, meaning someone up here very clever had removed the 30-calibre machine guns in the doorway and sent them to El Salvador, and someone just as clever down there had put the machine guns back in place. It appeared to me that this nation was marching rapidly toward another Vietnam-like tragedy."—DR. CHARLIE CLEMMENTS M.D.

"When the military first came, they would just ransack the houses. But later, this became more frequent and people were killed. They started burning houses, children, our granaries and our clothes. They even burned people.

"When we saw that they were killing children, tearing children apart, and the men and old people; that's when we became frightened and ran into the mountains to starve. After that they started to bring in the airplanes and helicopters."— "MARIA ELENA," San Jose de La Montana Refugee Camp, San Salvador.

In the shaded, icily air-conditioned Intelligence room, the G-2 drew back a curtain revealing a large-scale wall map of the region. One area was peppered with white map pins, another with red ones.

> *"What do the pins represent?"*
> "The red ones indicate that everyone in that area has gone, is dead, or will be dead once we have sanitized it."
> *"And the white ones...?"*
> "The white pins mean that the area has already been sanitized."

> "My niece was breast-feeding her eight-month-old baby when the army came. They tore the child from her arms and then they stood her on a stool—and they shot her dead."— "SOFIA," San Jose de la Montana Refugee Camp, San Salvador

The seeds of todays war were sown in 1932 in what became known as the *"Matanza"*—The Slaughter.

In 1931 El Salvador held its first and, many would say, last really free election. Hitherto the country had been run by a series of governments and dictators all of whom were nothing more than window dressing for the oligarchy of thirty-five families who controlled virtually every aspect of agricultural, commercial and political life. These men were the coffee barons whose ancestors stole land from the Pipil Indians at the time of the Spanish conquest to turn El Salvador by the nineteenth century into one of the world's major coffee producers. As far as the oligarchy were concernd the country and its people were theirs to do with as they pleased.

So poor were the people and so stark was the contrast between their life and that of the oligarchs that in 1931 the U.S. attaché to Central America remarked:

> "About the first thing one observes when he goes to San Salvador is the number of expensive automobiles on the streets. There seems to be nothing but Packards and Pierce-Arrows about. There appears to be nothing between these high-priced cars and the oxcart with its barefoot attendant. There is practically no middle class. Thirty or forty families own nearly everything in the country. They live in almost regal style. The rest of the population has practically nothing."

Major Harris went on to say:

> "I imagine the situation in El Salvador today is very much like France was before its revolution, Russia before its revolution and Mexico before its revolution...."

Finally he commented:

> "A socialist or communist revolution in El Salvador may be delayed for
> several years, ten or twenty, but when it comes it will be a bloody one."[1]

Why, oh why do politicians never learn? As with Archimedes Patti, Major
Harris's warning was, it would appear, ignored. The answer to calls for
revolution is to abolish those injustices that drive people to take up arms, not
to increase them. Hunger can only be cured with food; violent oppression will
eventually always produce armed revolt.

In the thirties, angered poverty-stricken peasants, left with no alternative
in order to bring about economic and political reform, were sending shock
waves of revolution through the length and breadth of the Central American
isthmus. In Nicaragua Sandino was prepared to die for it and to the north
Mexico had undergone its revolution, albeit the peasants did not believe it was
finished, nor do they now.

However, the oligarchs were too selfish to change and too stupid to see
that, without change, eventually they would lose everything. They thought that
an illusion of change was all that was needed; a safety valve which would
release the building pressure for revolution. Thus an election was announced.
They expected and planned for a junta of three army officers to romp home but
to their horror a democratic socialist, Alberto Araujo, who dreamed of forming
a Labor Party like that in Britain, took up the race. Because the elections had
been promoted as "free" and Araujo's popularity was so instant, the oligarchy
was unable to stop him. Peasants, workers, students, urban professionals and
intellectuals supported his plan for "the vital minimum" for all. As the election
drew closer, rumors began flying that should Araujo win, the oligarchy would
order a coup.

Election day arrived, votes were cast, ballots were counted and Araujo had
indeed won; the nation held its breath. But the military, whom the oligarchy
treated with a certain disdain, regarding them as no more than their own
praetorian guard, was producing a new breed of younger, more educated and
politically astute officers. The people had had their election, it had been as fair
as it could have been and they had chosen a leader. For the time being, at
least, the army would watch and wait; they would remain in their barracks.

A state of euphoria swept across the nation, but it was short lived; Araujo
couldn't deliver. His vague ideas of land reform were unworkable and as the
oligarchs removed their administrators from the civil service his party workers
moved in to fill the administrative vacuum; the result was chaos. They
implemented virtually none of Araujo's manifesto; instead, seduced by their
newfound power and the example of their predecessors, they set about lining
their own pockets. The effects on the economy were shattering. Inflation
soared. Food shortages grew. Coffee prices hit rock bottom. There was no work,

not even for the seasonal coffee pickers. Whatever Araujo had hoped to do had failed. The people felt they had been betrayed and angry demonstrations demanding food and work flared up all over the country.

At about this time Augustin Farabundo Marti, known, because of his exceedingly dark skin, as *El Negro Marti,* had returned from exile in Mexico and Nicaragua, where he had been a colonel in Sandino's army.

Though the two men fought side by side, Marti assuming the role of Sandino's secretary, their ideological differences were considerable. Marti, the son of a well-to-do farmer from La Libertad province, had been a Trotskyite revolutionary since his days at the university in San Salvador, whereas Sandino remained principally a nationalist and staunchly anti-imperialist.

> "My break with Sandino was not, as is sometimes said, for divergence of moral principles or opposing norms of conduct.... He would not embrace my communist program. His banner was only that of national independence...not social revolution. I solemnly declare that General Sandino is the greatest patriot in the world."—AUGUSTIN FARABUNDO MARTI, July 1929[2]

Since his return from exile Marti had been working as a representative of International Red Aid, a support organization for the communist workers' movement. Such organizations had sprung up all over the world since 1917, inspired by the Russian revolution. But El Salvador is just a speck on the map thousands of miles from the Soviet Union and links with Moscow were, as they are today, extremely tenuous.

In the countryside Marti's talk of a new egalitarian state with communal lands immediately struck a chord with the peasants, most of whom were whole or at least part Indian. Their memories were long. They knew that that was how it had been before the Spanish and the oligarchs. Marti and his people talked of a socialist state where people would work set hours, would have the right to form trade unions, to strike; where there would be free education for all and an end to discrimination against both Indians and women.

This was too much for the army. Elections and vague allusions to economic and agrarian reform were fine, but Marti was talking revolution and revolution jeopardized the oligarchy; and anything that jeopardized the oligarchy threatened the army. The country was about to explode, so it fell back on what even today, in this region of aristocrats and their dictators and generals, is the traditional remedy—a coup d'etat. Its leader was the vice-president, General Maximiliano Hernandez Martinez.

Throughout the country the Communists and Trade Unionists urged for insurrection, but although in just a few months Marti had become a symbol of an alternative, a hero, his communists were by no means able to assume leadership of the many and varied groups who were calling for an uprising.

Possibly for just that reason, all that they dreamed of came to nothing but carnage.

It was planned that the Indian peasants would march on certain towns where, they thought, the workers would immediately strike and the young army officers and troops who had shown such restraint during the post-election period would also join their cause. However, owing to the lack of a cohesive leadership and a fragmented organization, word of the impending uprising reached Martinez. The order went out to find Marti and bring him in. The same fate that would befall his friend Sandino happened to Marti. He was shot by firing squad and buried in an unmarked grave. And as the peasants reached the towns the army was waiting for them. Immediately four thousand were killed; anyone suspected of involvement was cut down where he was found. But this slaughter wasn't enough for the oligarchy. They would show these peasants, these Indians, who had dared to challenge them just whose country it was. They informed Martinez that they wanted revenge and he obliged with the *"Matanza"*—The Slaughter.

From the voting registers of the recent election they gleaned the names of members of the Communist Party. All but a few were killed in the massacres that swept through the country. In all, 30,000 peasants, many totally unconnected with the uprising, were murdered.[3] One report from the time revealed that the roads were littered with bodies as the National Guard butchered anyone they met. Such was the rapidity and extent of the killing the corpses couldn't be buried fast enough and "a great stench of rotting flesh permeated the air of western El Salvador."[4]

The scar left by the Matanza was so deeply etched in the hearts of ordinary Salvadorans that, though outwardly submissive, they could never forget it. For the next forty or so years, while living in conditions of extreme poverty, industrial workers and peasants alike held on to the dream that one day they might be rid of the oligarchy and their colonels. But as one corrupt government followed another, and more coups installed more presidents and juntas which proclaimed yet more new plans for reform, nothing actually changed.

For almost twenty years until October 1979 the Party of National Conciliation (P.C.N), a vehicle for the army and again a front for the oligarchy, held power. Through cheating and coercion they romped home in every election.

However, through the sixties and into the early seventies opposition groups began to form and gained prominence, representing every political hue from the Christian Democrats of Napoleon Duarte to all manner of Socialist and Communist factions. Worker and peasant organizations mushroomed in towns, cities and throughout the countryside, drawing support not simply from the masses but also from urban professionals, intellectuals and, most importantly, the church, hitherto an ally of the oligarchy but fast awakening to the philosophy of Liberation Theology. Men like Father Rutilio Grande, who was gunned down by the armed forces in March 1977, were using the scriptures to show the deeply religious peasants that God was not on the side of the oligarchs. All were calling even louder for reform.

As a reaction to the growth of these mass organizations, the *Organizacion Democratica Nacionalista,* popularly known by the acronym ORDEN (which in Spanish means order), was created by General Jose Alberto Medrano. It was a part-time paramilitary organization of up to 50,000 soldiers and small-holder peasants and was, according to Medrano, "the body and bones of the army in the countryside."[5] Its sole purpose was to help keep the PCN and its various presidents in power and thereby maintain the supremacy of the oligarchy by instilling terror in the minds of the peasants. This was achieved quite simply by torturing and killing members of the mass organizations. For many peasants, joining ORDEN was the only way to avoid becoming one of its victims, and at a time when all over El Salvador families were being forced into debt and off their few acres, the promises of credit to enable those who did join to maintain their land was hard to resist. Controlled by the Ministry of Defense, ORDEN never appeared on any ministry's budget and was accountable for its actions to no one but the president.[6]

During this period the number of landless peasants leaped from 11 percent in 1961 to a staggering 40 percent by 1975.[7]

"I knew a lot in an abstract way about El Salvador before I went there. That the average caloric intake is 1740 a day, about two-thirds of what it takes to sustain a human being. That 25 percent of all children die before age five. But it was within moments in a prenatal clinic that I came to understand that in a human dimension. A woman named Camilla—I would come to know her well—was a patient in the midst of her eighth pregnancy. I said, 'How many children do you have living?' She said, 'Three.' I asked, 'How many abortions or miscarriages?' She said, 'One.' I asked a medical question of what happened to the others, meaning had there been birth defects or pre-natal problems, and as she recovered from the anguish that that question provoked, she recited a litany I would hear from two to three thousand other women of child-bearing age. How her older son died in a year of too much rain; the next son died in a year of a drought; the third child in a year that the fertilizer prices doubled. The stories of people who live on 50 percent of what they produce, paying the rest to the landlord or lender—'Who could survive in a good year?' Meaning a quarter of all the children died. Or in a bad year they faced the difficulty: pay the landlord or lender what was due and watch another child grow hungry? Or feed the children one more year and watch their land be repossessed? And watch land that grew corn or beans or sorghum, then become expropriated as part of a hacienda or finca and be planted with coffee or cotton or sugar cane or be laid fallow to graze cattle. It was that process by which hundreds of thousands of peasants lost their land in El Salvador in the 1960s and '70s and set the stage for the revolution today."—Dr. Charlie Clemments, M.D.

During the mid to late seventies as the opposition parties challenged the right of the P.C.N. to continued rule, the four small armed groups of the center and left, representing differing ideologies and often antagonistic towards each other, materialized and in reaction to the atrocities of ORDEN began their random attacks against military installations and the Establishment. Composed primarily of members of the mass organizations who had had to go into hiding from the military and ORDEN, the guerrillas were not much in evidence before the late seventies. However, once they had appeared and since they were all that stood between the people and the military, their actions soon established them as the *"Muchachos"* (The Boys) in their respective regions, vesting in them certain territorial indentity.

> "My sons came to me and said 'Mama you're going to be alone now, we have to go away.' And that's when it all started. There was talk about how some peoples' documents were taken and people disappearing. Some of them would be found dead by the petrol station. Some of the 'Muchachos' wouldn't let the Guards into the village and that's how it started, that's how they started to protect us."— "Christina," San Jose de la Montana Refugee Camp, San Salvador

The reaction of the oligarchy to the growing national unrest was more violence meted out by ORDEN, and a new phenomenon to El Salvador, but not to Central America, the Death Squads.

Modeled on the Guatemalan example, these *Escuadrones de Muerte* were made up of members of the police, national guard, army and "the very sick young sons of affluent Salvadorans."[8] Using names such as The White Warriors Union, The Anticommunist Forces of Liberation and The Maximiliano Hernandez Martinez Brigade (the man who instigated the *Matanza* in 1932), they were purportedly controlled by Major Roberto D'Aubuisson. At the time D'Aubuisson was Assistant Chief of Intelligence and later, while continuing to direct the Death Squads, he founded the extreme right wing party ARENA. As leader of ARENA, and with the backing of the United States ambassador, D'Aubuisson became for a time President of the National Assembly. He is said to have proposed 'the complete annihilation of the left along the lines of 1932,' and his general secretary of ARENA said, "We don't believe the army needs controlling. We are fighting a war and civilians will be killed. They have always been. It has got to be that way."[9]

> "All the men have had to carry arms because of the massacres; and because of the atrocities against the children. I was caught in one of the massacres and saw a whole family whose children had been decapitated. I don't believe it was the 'Muchachos' who started it. They had to pick up their weapons

183

and fight to protect what they have; their mothers, their children and everything that belongs to them."— "Patricia," San Jose de la Montaña Refugee Camp, San Salvador

"When people went into town, their goods would be taken away from them for no apparent reason. Sometimes they would take the men, and they would disappear."— "Christina," San Jose de la Montana Refugee Camp, San Salvador

Paid well for their grizzly nocturnal work by members of the oligarchy, by 1986 the Death Squads had murdered over 60,000 peasants, factory workers, union officials, teachers, doctors, students and human rights workers.[10]

"We lived peacefully. But we were controlled by them, by the rich. We worked, we used to sell our produce. But when we wanted to change the way we lived, that's when truckloads of soldiers started to come. We became afraid to go to Suchitoto. People started to disappear, one here, one there. People became frightened to go to town to sell, and so they couldn't get any money to buy anything to eat."— "Cecilia," San Jose de la Montaña Refugee Camp, San Salvador

El Salvador sank into actual civil war sometime between the October 1979 coup, which finally ended the near twenty-year rule of the P.C.N. and April 1980. Led by young officers who realized, too late, that reform was imperative, the coup brought civilian representatives from the opposition and intelligentsia into the new ruling junta. The Christian Democrats, Social Democrats, the Communist Party, and a renegade progressive oligarchy all realized that this was possibly the last chance for peaceful change. But such was the entrenchment of the oligarchs and senior officers, especially Colonel Garcia, the clean-cut and ruthless new Minister of Defense, that once more no reforms of any substance happened and the military and Death Squads continued to murder at will.

Despite the fact that the civilians on the junta were representative of a whole spectrum of centerist and moderate left wing thinking, the oligarchy regarded them all as simply extremists and leftists. At the turn of the year the junta members representing these factions, led by the Social Democrat Guillermo Unog, issued an ultimatum: either Garcia goes, or we go. Of course, Garcia remained at his post and the majority of the civilians resigned on January 3, 1980. Once out of government many of them were driven underground where they united to form the Democratic Revolutionary Front (F.D.R.), becoming the political representatives of the guerrillas and bringing the four major armed groups together under one command, uniting in the memory of the martyr of 1932—The Farabundo Marti Front for National Liberation (F.M.L.N.).

The final straw came in March. The outspoken Archbishop Oscar Romero, a courageous and tireless champion of the people who once said of his life in El Salvador, "My job seems to be to go around picking up insults and corpses,"[11] delivered a sermon in the Cathedral of San Salvador on Sunday, March 23. As usual it was fiery and uncompromising and ended with this direct appeal to the army:

> "Brothers, each one of you is one of us. We are the same people. The campesinos you kill are your own brothers and sisters. When you hear the words of a man telling you to kill, remember instead the words of God, 'thou shalt not kill.' God's law must prevail. No soldier is obliged to obey an order contrary to the law of God. It is time that you come to your senses and obey your conscience rather than follow a sinful command. The Church, defender of the rights of God, the law of God and the dignity of each human being, cannot remain silent in the presence of such abominations. We should like the government to take seriously the fact that reforms dyed with so much blood are worthless. In the name of God, in the name of our tormented people who have suffered so much and whose laments cry out to heaven, I beseech you, I beg you, I order you…in the name of God, stop the repression!"

Less than twenty-four hours later, in the small chapel of the Divine Providence Hospital, Archbishop Romero delivered another sermon and having finished he turned to the congregation, "Let us pray."…Before they could kneel Archbishop Romero was dead, killed instantly by a bullet fired from the silenced gun of a hired assassin.

Six days later as the people of San Salvador joined to bury their archbishop, a bomb was thrown outside the cathedral and snipers opened fire on the congregation. Twenty-six of them were killed and over two hundred wounded. The war had begun.

The army became more brutal, the Death Squads more murderous, the guerrillas more daring, the junta and subsequent governments more intransigent, refusing to negotiate with the F.D.R., and the people more frightened. The whole sorry pattern that was predicted in 1931 by Major Harris, and counterparts of which have raged through the Americas, Africa and Asia, is being repeated yet again, and yet again the U.S. is becoming deeply involved—with the wrong side—justifying its actions with rhetorical declamations about Havana- and Moscow-inspired communism, this time "in our backyard" and the necessity to protect "our vital vested interests."

> "The Cuban vice president, Carlos Rafael Rodriguez, and I met in Mexico City.…It was not my intention to threaten or intimidate Rodriguez.…I simply wanted him to understand, without equivocation, how the Reagan Administration viewed the situation in El Salvador, and I wanted to suggest

to him, as truthfully as possible, what measures the United States might take *to defend its interests* and preserve the government in El Salvador."— GENERAL ALEXANDER HAIG (*Caveat*). (Emphasis added.)

"If the United States was to recognize that there are fundamental injustices, that there is a dung heap of poverty and injustice that exist there that force people into a revolutionary mode, if they were to recognise that then they would then also have to be admitting that in many instances they're on the side of the black hats. They're supporting the bad guys and they're supporting the right of the privileged to spread death throughout Latin America. But they can't acknowledge that so what they have to do is to suggest that this is a fundamental part of the east-west struggle—this is a fundamental area of competition between Marxism and the United States, and that is *not* an accurate portrayal."—CONGRESSMAN GEORGE MILLER

"The vast majority of the Salvadorans I lived with couldn't tell you Marx Groucho from Karl, but they do understand the reality of the struggle and what they're striving for, and that is an inspiration that was largely the result of liberation theology. In the 1960s and 70s the poorest of all of Latin Americans began to understand that their misery wasn't the result of God's will so much as a few mens' greed."—DR. CHARLIE CLEMMENTS

At least one million people have been forced from their homes by the war. That represents fully 20 percent of the population; a higher percentage than in Vietnam at the height of that war. Five hundred thousand have fled the country in fear, but the other half million, mainly women and children and old men, are crammed into makeshift camps often provided by the church in San Salvador.[1]

"We were about four families who came here together yesterday. Every day they send planes to bomb, and probably tonight they will too. We can't be there because we have children. We didn't have food or houses any more— nothing. Even our clothes are not our own, they were given to us. We have come here and luckily they have helped us. They have given us shelter, food, milk for the children. We want to go back to our own land. We can't, there is nothing left, no food....We feel happier here but even so we're still afraid. We're afraid they'll come here and kill us here because they weren't able to do it there. Sometimes they tell us that."— "SONIA," San Jose de la Montaña Refugee Camp, San Salvador

"Over there they're bombing night and day. When I start to cook tortillas or wash clothes, suddenly they come and you have to leave everything and run. If you don't watch it, you're dead. The other day, on Sunday, seven people died. I believe it was four children and three adults, one of whom was pregnant. They couldn't get out of the way and they were hit."— "ALICIA"

The war has denuded the rural towns and villages of their populations, leaving many of them now little more than garrisons. Not far from the town of Aguilares, where Rutilio Grande was shot, Suchitoto sits like a sugar topping on a hill overlooking Lake Suchitlan. In the center of the town, white as cake

frosting, the mandatory church shimmers on the eastern side of a square from
which long cobbled streets lined with single-storey, boarded-up homes in
white, faded green and bleached-out pink run in fingers down the hill to the
no-man's-land beyond. From the shadows under the covered sidewalk on the

southern side of the square comes the measured regular thud of a soldier's boot on flagstones and somewhere opposite a "clack!" as a shell is smacked into the breach of an M16. In the distance a peasant woman pats out her tortillas and slaps them on to an oil-drum lid that serves as her stove and from the direction of Aguilares a couple of Guardia, their lacquer black steel helmets matching their mirrored sunglasses, strut into the square, steel tipped jack boots striking sparks from the cobbles. One of the two civilians gets up from his place by the stone bench in the center of the square, stretches his hind legs, then front, and trots off, his tongue dripping, in search of shade. Twelve thousand people used to live here; seven thousand have fled.

Beside the church a gang of maybe twenty old men painstakingly re-lay a cobbled street, inset into which are parallel tracks of special concrete pavings just about the right width to carry armored vehicles smoothly through the town. The work is being paid for by U.S. AID.

"We get six *colones* a day," said the man who called himself Miguel. He was fifty-six and looked seventy. "If we are lucky we might get ten days' work out of this this month. That's sixty *colones,* but I have to pay thirty to the landlord for our home.... There's no other work for us, not in the fields any more, it's too dangerous... and I don't even like to go out there to get firewood. If they see you, they shoot at you because they think you are with the Muchachos." He bent his brittle back to pick up another cobble and deliver it to the mason. Sixty *colones* is equal to about $15.

Down in the valley on the outskirts of the town a hot wind cuts through the overgrowth, scratching the uneasy silence. This is no-man's-land, overseen constantly by vultures whose black overstuffed bodies crowd awkwardly onto trees as gnarled as the people who used to welcome their shade. Barely discernible beneath the untended banana palms and tamarinds, roofless shell-pocked ruins offer a headless doll, a holed kettle or occasionally a faded photograph face down in the dirt as the only evidence that these were once homes. Away from the potholed road spattered with red painted slogans of the Muchachos, up dusty tracks that lead nowhere anymore, a lone family cling on, living defiantly beneath a soldier's graffiti: "Long live the tyrany of the armed forces."

"When did they paint that?"
"Last week."
"Did they do anything else?"
"No—we have nothing to break anymore."
"Do they often come here?"
"All the time."
"Aren't you frightened?"
"Yes. But mostly we hide in the campo."
"So why don't you leave?"
"Where can we go? This is our home."
"Will you stay then?"
"Maybe. It depends."
"On what?"
"On them, the soldiers and that man, what's his name...you know, the one who gives the guns to them...you know...the Yankee...he's the President or something like that."

Walking back to the road, a line from a song by Gill Scott Heron keeps running though my mind: "You go give those liberals hell, Ronnie...call in the cavalry to disrupt this perception of freedom gone wild. God damn it, first one wants freedom, then the whole damn world wants it."

By the burned-out Texaco station overgrown with tinder-dry grass, if it weren't for the rusted old sign on which Suchitoto is barely discernible among the bullet holes a stranger would hardly know the town lay ahead. The army would like to keep it that way. They and the Guardia hold Suchitoto and its inhabitants, "protecting" them from their fathers and sons, the Muchachos, out there somewhere beyond no-man's-land.

"Everything is quiet, *tranquilo,* there's no story here for you" said the Guardia teniente with ice-grey eyes. "Everything is safe, *Todo tranquilo.*"

"Oh, yes, safe for them. They might be relaxed in the town but in the *campo* (countryside) it's terrible. On the 7th we moved because there were soldiers everywhere—we fled on foot. On that day I was very sick and weak. I don't usually get sick but it's the malnutrition. On that day I thought I was going to die.... We heard they were coming down to Chaparral from Suchitoto. ...We know they captured one man who was sweeping—but we don't know what happened to him. The children can't even stand. They are all yellow; look at me. Everyone's in bad shape...they keep us in a circle of terror."
— "ALICIA"

"Ninety percent of the guerrillas in Guazapa were born and raised there, the others were from other parts of El Salvador and the civilians chose to live in an area that was bombed or rocketed or strafed daily or overrun by government soldiers in "search and destroy" operations. They *chose* to live there rather than live in other parts of the country where a Death Squad may knock on your door in the middle of the night and carry you away."— DR. CHARLIE CLEMMENTS

Life in the mountains is hard even without the bombing. Food is scarce and in the dry season people go for months at a time literally on beans and tortillas, nothing else. Sometimes *El Norte,* the icy wind that blows down from Mexico for days at a stretch, is so cold that it can take two hours, even in the blistering tropical sun, to drive the chill from their bones in the morning. No one who has seen the conditions and talked to the people can accuse either the *Muchachos* or civilians of not knowing why they are there. The commitment necessary to endure the life is more than most comfortable westerners would be able to muster. These are not mindless peasants, brainwashed by demonic "Communists" from far away. They are ordinary people who understand perfectly their situation and choose it since no other course of action is left for them. None of them wants to fight, none of them wants to lie in their hammocks at night listening to the steady ominous drone of U.S. surveillance aircraft bristling with heat sensors and infra-red gadgets that pin-point bodies and portend another rocketing tomorrow or maybe napalm. None of them is here because they enjoy it, except maybe the children, who like their counterparts in West Beirut, have known little else and so long as they have their mothers, feel secure—except when the bombs fall. Then you see the wide eyes and whitened skin of fear.

"The massacres have been the worst thing. People's eyes being gouged out with pins; people being slowly tortured till they killed them piece by piece. All the people that were maimed and decapitated.

"The massacres they caused with the bombings. When a bomb falls and the shrapnel flies it kills hundreds of children and adults at the same time and it kills all the trees. Everything is destroyed."— "PATRICIA"

"Lyndon Johnson during the early stages of the Vietnam War said it's ridiculous to suppose that a tenth-rate Asian power can challenge the United States. And there was this sense that a detachment of Marines could change the political balance in a Third World country, particularly in a Latin American setting.

"We're now engaged in Central America trying to somehow find a high technology military fix to smash yet another national revolution, with tragic results, I think—both for ourselves and for the country that is involved in the process. You can kill a lot of people, but you can't change the political course of events."—PROFESSOR RICHARD FALK

"I think there are some strong parallels between Central America and South East Asia as I knew it. There are similarities in tactics; of 'Scorched Earth,' of 'Search and Destroy' operations, of 'Free Fire Zones.' A Free Fire Zone, for example, means an area in which any living thing is a legitimate target and it was my congressional testimony that led Colonel Bustillo to exclaim: 'Yes, Guazapa's a free-fire zone,' meaning any of the 16 clinics or any of the two hospitals, any of the 30 schools were legitimate targets, in addition to the 10,000 civilians—40% of whom are under age 12. The use of white phosphorus, a heinous weapon that's used to mark 'fixed targets'—that's the way the military describes it—white phosphorus burns at about 200 degrees Centigrade. It penetrates skin quite readily because it coagulates connective tissue—skin, fat. It smoulders long after initial contact and can often spontaneously reignite so someone in the hospital can begin smouldering if the wound hasn't been adequately debreeded. White phosphorus was used every day on an indiscriminate basis the last six months I was there. It was denied by U.S. military advisers, by the U.S. Embassy for almost a full year, but recently a U.S. Embassy spokesperson admitted that white phosphorus was used but only 'to mark fixed targets.'

"Five-year-old Freddy, who was one of my last patients there, was in a 'fixed target' known as his home, when his twelve-year-old sister was killed in the same attack. Fixed targets mean hospitals, clinics and schools."—Dr. CHARLIE CLEMMENTS

In 1984 as part of the ever-increasing U.S. military assistance program (MAP) an innocent-looking but lethal plane known as an AC-47 Gunship was delivered to the Salvadoran Air Force. In Vietnam it earned the nicknames "Spooky" and "Puff, the Magic Dragon" because its guns can splatter up to eighteen thousand rounds of high calibre ammunition a minute over vast tracts of land. The Reagan Administration pledged to Congress that only one plane would be sent. However, a report which was co-authored by Congressman Miller revealed that the pledge, like so many others, had been broken, and that "in fact, a second gunship went into battle on the same day that the first was initially deployed."[13]

"For the most part you have to understand that most members of Congress did not know that those gunships were being introduced into El Salvador. They did not know certainly that there was more than one gunship in use and that there was anticipation that there would be others to follow and they simply don't appreciate what that means in terms of the widening of the war. None of them realize that we've dumped almost $2 billion into the Salvadoran military effort and into the Salvadoran economy because they don't realize how many times they've voted to expand the war in Salvador. We're calling, out of necessity, for greater and greater American involvement in this war because the technology outstrips the ability of the Salvadorans to govern their own war, and what we now see and what the report points to

210

clearly is three things: We are financing almost the entire operation, in Salvador; we're responsible for widening the type of war that exists in El Salvador, and now what we're doing is…clearly getting deeper and deeper involved in terms of American personnel and American know-how to keep that war effort running. And so what you see in the end is that we have basically an American subsidized military response to the social and economic problems in El Salvador. It's just as we saw in Vietnam. The vast amount of money that the President keeps referring to that he says they have labelled as economic aid is really being used to indirectly underwrite the military, and in fact only 15 percent is economic aid and they don't want to present that to the Congress. They feel much more comfortable coming up and saying that "our economic aid outweighs military by a ratio of two to one; we really care about the people of El Salvador." We care so much we turn our gunships loose on them."—Congressman George Miller

"Stop sending the aid! That's what I would say to President Reagan. Maybe his conscience should tell him because he's the father of a family and if he saw how we have had to bury our sons and families, like dogs…And sometimes we haven't been able to bury them at all. Wherever they fall and die, that's where they stay. Where our farms used to be, where the land was fertile, where we could produce things—now there is nothing, just craters where the bombs have fallen. And I think this has effected the economy of El Salvador because in the Frontline—that's what they call it, the Frontline of the war—but that's where our farms are.…I've seen them! I've seen the massacres, only families and old people and children. Twenty-six I've seen dead for three months, without being buried, rotting."— "Christina"

"When there was a massacre at Guadelupe near Tenango, that's when my father was wounded. We were walking in lines. First a helicopter flew overhead and then came the A-37s—the airplanes. It circled us, we were scared because we knew the army was close to us and if they caught us they would kill us all. We ran up towards the mountains through some roads, there was no cover. There were about ten airplanes; helicopters, Mustangs and A-37s. Many old people and children were killed there. This baby here was only three months old. I tried to put my children underneath the blood-soaked bodies. You see, I couldn't move because my father was wounded. Until they finished the bombing, I was sure I was going to die there too. The children were really dazed by all the bombing, shelling, even the smell. Two months later I was still a bit dazed, and my oldest son has a ruptured ear. It hasn't healed."—Maria Elena

On March 5, 1984, the infamous Atlacatl Battalion under the command of the late Colonel Domingo Monterosa began a sweep north from the garrison town of San Miguel into "G" (guerrilla) territory, as the U.S. advisers call it. At 5 a.m. on the morning of March 6 they surprised a small group of FMLN guerrillas passing through San Luis de la Reina, an impoverished village which represented home for a few peasants. The army attacked, the guerrillas retreated, and as so often happens, the civilians were caught in the cross-fire.

The little girl was shot through the spine. A medivac helicopter was called in and the girl together with a dead soldier and some other wounded were shipped back to San Miguel for medical attention. It is fairly safe to assume that had the incident not been witnessed by outsiders, the girl would probably not have been evacuated and the village might have paid an even greater price for selling food to the "Muchachos." As it was, Teniente Amaya handed out footballs to the few kids remaining in the village and talked of "winning hearts and minds"—I'm sure I've heard that before somewhere.

When the army eventually left and all was quiet once more, village boys would be instructed by their mothers to climb to the roofs of their homes and whistle friendly bird-like calls. "What's that for?" I asked. "To tell the Muchachos that it's safe to come back." It will take more than footballs to win these hearts and minds.

I tell this story for one reason only, it had an interesting post-script. Colonel Monterosa was a fearless soldier of great charm. He was always up at the front with his men and thus earned their respect; at least the respect of those who were themselves any good as soldiers; the majority, being very young farm kids, most of whom had been press-ganged into military service, were not. He was not somebody I would want as a friend but while he was ruthless and had, if not ordered, at least accepted the appalling acts that some of his men perpetrated, Monterosa was no one's fool. He had worked his way up through the military from quite humble beginnings unlike many of his counterparts, and therefore had an appreciation of the hardship of peasant life.

On the evening of March 5, sitting on the edge of a small flat-topped hill looking west to the sunset, he said:

> "We cannot win this war. I know I have been fighting it. We cannot win because what the guerrillas are promising the people, is what the people want and need. They need land, they need food, they need water and health care and electricity and schools and jobs. Until the government in San Salvador changes its attitude and can give them those things, the war will go on."

It was not the first time that the colonel had voiced such opinions, albeit quietly, but some say that holding them had made him enemies within certain sections of the military establishment.

Some months later he was killed when his helicopter was blown up shortly after takeoff en route to San Salvador. All that was recovered from the wreckage to show that he ever existed or made such liberal statements was his left upper-arm and pectoral still inside some tatters of his battle dress with MONTEROSA clearly visible on the blood-soaked name bar.

It was assumed that the F.M.L.N. were responsible, but no one has ever identified officially the mysterious officer who placed a black attaché case on the helicoptor shortly before takeoff, but did not himself take the ride.

"If the U.S. continues to annually increase the amounts of military assistance to El Salvador, I believe that the war will grind on in an attritive stalemate which further destroys the economic infrastructure and requires simultaneous increases in economic support funds to keep the country going as it is being destroyed."—EDWARD L. KING[14]

Edward King's statement is yet another echo of the Vietnam War. Of that action they said, "In order to save the country we will have to destroy it"! And what of Major Patti's "Communist Blinders"? Well they are also still being worn, but today it appears that they are accompanied by ear plugs.

Ever since their creation in 1980 the FDR recognized and continues to state that the solution to El Salvador's war is and always has been a just negotiated settlement including real reforms. Their proposals are clear-cut and realistic:

1. A direct sharing of power by the F.M.L.N./F.D.R. in a transition government that would include other political parties and representative political groups of the middle class and the private-enterprise sectors not tied to the oligarchy.

2. The purification of the army to include soldiers from the rebel army and some from the present army who have not been implicated in killings outside of combat.

3. A mixed economy with rigorous reforms in the agrarian sector, financed by foreign trade.

4. A nonaligned foreign policy, including a relationship of mutual respect with the United States, (The plan would also offer the United States as well as El Salvador's neighbors a reciprocal security treaty. The F.M.L.N/F.D.R. recognizes that the United States has legitimate security interests in the region.

5. The right of El Salvador to choose its own political development free of foreign interference.

6. Full rights of trade-union organization and assembly, respect for human rights, and freedom of expression and movement.[15]

Neither side can win a military victory. But neither the Salvadoran government nor the U.S. seems to hear these proposals for peace. Although there have been a couple of well publicized meetings between the FDR leaders and President Duarte, neither his govenment nor the U.S. Embassy seems in any hurry to contine the negotiations.

"Fred Ikle, the third-ranking man in the Defense Department, has stated very clearly: 'We seek a military victory for the forces of democracy' in El Salvador. I think there's no doubt that they somehow perceive that they can militarily control the situation. The United States is totally controlling the situation. In fact Salvadoran military officers admitted a year ago they don't make a decision without turning to their U.S. counterparts."—DR. CHARLIE CLEMMENTS

What I think has been so difficult for American leadership to comprehend is that nationalism in its contemporary form is a very strong political force and one that isn't susceptible to just being smashed by high technology military power. You can kill a lot of people but you can't change the political course of events, and I think that's been extremely hard to accept as a condition of the modern world. One sees it all over the world in recent history—the Vietnam War's of course the most dramatic example, but the Soviet Union is facing the same kind of reality in Afghanistan."—PROFESSOR RICHARD FALK

"After more than two billion dollars of military aid, after technological innovations and escalation, with AC-47 gunships, with AC-130 radar ships that provide Intelligence information, with A-37 fighter attack bombers, with tanks, we have yet to understand why '*their* Salvadorans fight better than *our* Salvadorans,' as our State Department would put it; and the fact that we're relying upon 15- to 17-year-old Salvadorans who President Duarte admitted are drafted at gunpoint, who have no stake in the sytem they're defending. They're very much like the American GI in Vietnam in 1970. Their goal in life is to stay alive for a year. Compare that to a young person— a 15- to 17-year-old—that feels like he or she is defending their family, struggling for an existence, to establish a new system of social justice and whose determination in battle will mean the safety of their loved ones, and you have the beginning of why U.S. foreign policy will never work. We cannot buy morale, we cannot buy leadership nor can we end corruption with millions of U.S. dollars, and we have failed to understand that in Central America as badly as we did South East Asia."—DR. CHARLIE CLEMMENTS

"You know, the tragedy is we're going to destroy each and every one of these countries and the problems of poverty are going to go away, the guerrilla problem is not going to go away, and when we're all said and done, we'll be right back where we were twenty-five years ago."—CONGRESSMAN GEORGE MILLER

El Salvador

"Why do intelligent people keep doing the same dumb things? At least that's one way of looking at American foreign policy. These repeated interventions against radical nationalist movements that are very draining in terms of resources, that don't succeed in terms of political goals and that split the domestic society very deeply at home. Why do we keep doing it? What is the compulsion that leads us to keep doing it?"—PROFESSOR RICHARD FALK

PART TWO

"The Masters of War"

In early fall on alternate years a bizarre event takes place at Farnborough and Paris. From all over the world apparently respectable people—politicians, military personnel and sleek-suited salesmen—forgather to pass four or five days meeting old friends, making new ones, talking shop and consuming inordinate amounts of free food and champagne. The public, who do not get the free booze, are also encouraged to join in the fun of these events under the illusion that they are attending an "Air Show." But the term Air Show is in fact simply a euphemism for what is nothing less than an immaculately produced sales convention for our most immoral manufacturers—the arms makers.

Nineteen eighty-four was a Farnborough year. The genteel manicured order of the Surrey countryside was shattered as the F-20 Tigershark and others of its breed rent the still English air and men with clipped voices reminiscent of Battle of Britain fighter aces delivered inane commentaries to entertain the punters and distract them from the real business of the day.

> "Magic, Matra Magic Air to Air missiles can be carried on the outboard stations and the effective use of the missiles is ensured by a highly elaborate inertial nav-attack system...with head-up display and lazer telemetry...the object of the improvements giving much better air combat performance and increasing what is now called 'survivability' in air to ground operations. Don't see how you can increase that 'survivability'; either you live or you don't."—Official commentary, Farnborough Air Show, 1984

In the deep carpeted sales chalets and tents, heady with the scent of expensive flower arrangements, the champagne bubbled and glasses chinked; sights, sounds and smells that were quite different from those at the Green Line in Beirut or the dusty trails and dense forests of El Salvador. The merchants, generals and government representatives viewed seductive promotion videos and talked easily of deals worth tens of millions while just a few hours flying time away people were dying for want of a $7,000 ambulance to take them to the hospital that would administer a $70 drug and dress a wound with a 70-cent bandage.

Outside, the fighter planes and attack helicopters continued to perform their aerial dance of death, and with every fly past, every roll and screaming jet, press cameras clicked and whirred to capture the evil beauty; and Margaret Thatcher came to visit.

With polite disinterest she swept by the products of our partners in the European Community; Mrs. Thatcher believes, it would appear, the traditional British saying that "all wogs start at Dover" and dislikes Europeans.

"Eleven-o-Five the P.M. will be at the Oto Melara Stand (Italian), then down aisle C to meet the people on the Giat stand (French); at Eleven-o-Seven and at Eleven-o-Eight the P.M. will move on to the Shorts Brothers stand (British)..." the P.R. man rattled until he had completed the minute-by-minute itinerary. "Shouldn't really be giving you this info ahead of time you know, security and all that. Don't tell the police I told you.... By the way," he asked with a laugh, "you're not with the I.R.A. are you?"

Mrs. Thatcher did stop at the Shorts Brothers exhibit, where she learned of the virtues of one of their lethal products and with dollar signs illuminating that surgically produced smile she announced to the assembled press: "We've got an order for this one," and the Cameras clicked and caught every plastic nuance.

"There's a lot of coverage by the Press of the military and what it develops and the latest products and how well they work, almost as though that were all it was, you know, a product. Then of course people who know what we have and are aware of what it can do or at least of what we say it can do— there's often quite a difference—mesh that with what they think their needs are or what we tell them their needs are."

"Do you think that there is an understanding among the salesmen of what happens when somebody pulls the trigger on one of these things."

"No I don't think they think about that at all."—Tom Gervasi, Director, Center for Military Research

"At the moment, as you see, you've got some medium-range air-to-air missiles for which you would need the appropriate, appropriately capable radar, which the aircraft could be fitted with. You've also got the Magique short-range air-to-air missile and that could be used on the aircraft as could Sidewinder 9L or for that matter for short-range purposes there's also the advance short-range air-to-air missile which you see over there, which again is an alternative when it comes into being for the aircraft.

"The orange ones are ordinary ballistic bombs. They are free-fall bombs. Any operator has to decide on the type of targets that he's going after, which weapon to best use. A bomb or series of bombs, a cluster of bombs for instance—I should say a "range" or "stick of bombs"—would be used perhaps against large buildings and things of that sort, where you've got to...spread the damage. If you want to concentrate a little bit more, then perhaps you'd use a group of rockets...you've got these small rockets here. With a dedicated ballistic weapon, you almost must hit what you're aiming at but with something like these smaller weapons you spread and you aim at an area instead of a specific target. There's a fairly large one in there— American as well, again a rocket—it spreads the area. To lose off a number of rockets is a similar effect to cluster bombs. You have much smaller explosives but spread in an area instead of having the larger explosive concentrated in one point.... So the ability of the aircraft to carry weapons has been improved. The weight of weapons that can be carried has been increased and the wide range of weapons that it can carry is quite impressive as you can see...."

(The man could be your local Ford dealer helping you decide whether you want the coupe or the drop head and what optional extras you should go for.)

> "That is a Cluster Bomb. The little propeller you see on the front unwinds the system and primes it and then a range of bomblettes come out.... The center section there are Brandt Baps. There are also Brandt Baps further along. It and the BL755 are cluster type weapons, to put a range of explosive devices in an area on the ground and...to therefore cover an area instead of aiming specifically at one target."—JOHN HUGHES, British Aerospace Salesman

Never at any time did Mr. Hughes or any of his colleagues mention, even in passing, the victims, and it is almost certain that none of them have ever witnessed the smashed or charred or limbless bodies or listened to their screams or tried to look their families in the eye.

> "I think that the use of language is very important because words imply moral categories and unfortunately much of the human dimension of warfare has been obscured in this new language. A free-fire zone, remember, means an area in which any living thing is a legitimate target, and having an aircraft attack you, firing 6,000 rounds a minute, dropping bombs perhaps of napalm or firing white phosphorus rockets, is an experience that's very difficult to understand until you are there. I had flown some of those aircraft as trainers— and I had watched them unload their destructive power in Vietnam, but until you're on the receiving end it's difficult to comprehend what it means and the fear it evokes."—DR. CHARLIE CLEMMENTS, M.D.

The merchants of death and their customers in the armed services have always had their own, rather awkward language which has sought to dehumanize everything. But in recent years this practice has reached the realms of lunacy. Why is it now necessary to call a good old-fashioned soldier's boot a "Leather Personnel Carrier"; or a noise, an "Acoustical Excitation." Though ludicrous and confusing, these terms don't set out to deceive, or disguise the object or phenomenon and therefore do no real harm, except possibly to our brains (not to mention the clarity of the English Language).

But the use of true euphemisms is an Orwellian aspect of the modern military machine and its suppliers which seeks increasingly to make the sale of conventional weapons and conventional wars more acceptable, since a nuclear war would be bad for business and therefore quite out of the question.

To achieve this acceptance the language has to be sterilized and constantly changed, added to and up-dated, which compounds the distancing and confusion. Remember what happened to Operation Hades? And napalm now has two "clean" names— "Selective" and, "Soft Ordnance." Doesn't even sound as if it burns, does it? But just in case it's politically too sensitive a situation to use napalm, under whatever name, there is even a substitute substance now with a name that suggests one could buy it in a pharmacy— "Incendigel."

Wars are no longer fought on "battlefields" by generals and their troops whose aim is to take and hold territory. Since that first dive-bombing raid on Sandino in 1928 the battlefields have increasingly been cities and towns, and a fundamental part of modern strategy therefore is to cause as much physical and emotional pain as possible, particularly to civilians. In the arsenals of the modern army there is a genus of weapons that has been designed not to kill but specifically to maim. They are usually quite small and when detonated hurl white hot shards of metal or ballbearings ripping through human flesh and bones. These delightful little gizmos are collectively known as anti-personnel grenades, cluster bomblettes and area denial weapons. The officially stated need for them is to deny the enemy access to tracts of land such as air fields by showering such areas with these tiny devices. But in reality they are dumped anywhere, the specific intention being to inflict greater numbers of serious casualties and thereby increase the pressure on medical teams and hospitals hard-pressed anyway to cope, thus adding to the enemy's demoralization.

I have often contemplated the minds of the men who dream up these devices. They are probably ordinary, maybe loving, husbands and fathers. Every morning they breakfast with the family, kiss their wives goodbye as they in turn wish them "a good day at work dear." They drop the kids off at school with more hugs and kisses and then head for a corporation for whom they pass all their creative working hours thinking up more devilish and cruel ways to hurt fellow human beings. They spend days over their designs, ensuring that they are precise down to the thousandth of an inch; they examine the beautifully manufactured, precision end product and then return to a warm home and loving family and continue as if they have been designing a labor-saving kitchen gadget. And since there are thousands of these people continuing their labors, one has to assume that they sleep exceptionally well, never even in their darkest dreams hearing the cries when one of their lovingly produced anti-personnel weapons is detonated.

Anti-personnel being of course a little too descriptive, these weapons also have clean names such as "Smartlettes," a "Frag" and the "Potato Masher." And while we're on the subject of food, the Cheeseburger is a slice of Americana that found its way over to Vietnam. But you can't eat it, it eats you. The Cheeseburger is the BLU/82/B11 concussion bomb. It is the most powerful non-nuclear bomb in our arsenals. It weights 7.5 tons, is eleven feet long and four feet six inches wide and sends a mushroom cloud six thousand feet into the air killing everything within 755 acres and almost everything within two thousand acres. In Vietnam you cannot find 750 to 2000 acres of land that is free of people, but the Cheeseburger was dropped regularly and without warning by U.S. bombers to instantly convert jungle and agricultural land into landing zones for helicopters. And it doesn't matter whatever name the BLU/82/B11 is christened—the Cheeseburger or, as someone with a really sick sense of humor in Vietnam named it, The Daisy Cutter—it still obliterates people.

The list of sanitized deceits goes on and on; for Free Fire Zone now read "Pre-Cleared-Zone." And remember that most cynical and cruel of deceptions from Vietnam, "Friendly Fire," which was, I assume, easier than saying, "Your son was killed by a bullet (or shell, or grenade or whatever) fired by his own side"; now it is even more obtuse— "Accidental Delivery." Oh, so innocent, isn't it; just sounds like the postman screwed up.

Finally, before we go completely mad, there is—Wargasm! Apparently it means "leading inevitably to a climax of war." All of these terms specifically intend to deceive; they attempt to make these obscene and uneconomic products appear more acceptable both to us and the men who use them.[1]

> "One goes back to the days when the fliers were flying over Vietnam and dropping bombs and didn't have any idea—and really I'm sure didn't want to know—exactly what those bombs were doing. There're very few military men who get off on knowing that they're wreaking destruction and that there's blood flowing down there and bits of bodies flying hither and...and they don't want to know that. They simply want to know that they have 'destroyed a target.' Today we are removing things even further. We have very, very high technology; we have 'smart weapons'; one day a man will sit in a basement of the Pentagon and he will look at a video screen and that screen will be showing him what a 'remotely piloted vehicle,' with no human being in it, sees as it flies over the Pyrenees, let us say, and looks down with its television camera. And he will see that there are some bodies and he will assume, since we all must interpret, that these bodies are 'hostile' and he will instruct that remotely piloted vehicle to release 'ordnance' on those 'personnel' who will then be destroyed, and he will 'have achieved a solution' and he will sit there as though he had been playing a video game.
>
> "The whole language of war is a form of denial. It is saying that we are not really doing what we are doing. We talk about 'Area Denial Weapons,' we talk about 'Anti-Personnel' weapons, we talk about all sorts of things in terms that sanitize and remove the agent from the result."—TOM GERVASI

The arms industry is not only rife with deceits and cynicism, it is also competitive and self-escalating. Every year new weapons appear doing just a little more than the last, and the enthusiasm to sell them seems inexhaustible. I calculate that Farnborough '84 cost the industry two hundred and fifty-two million dollars.[2] But this is a multi-billion-dollar industry and two hundred and fifty-two million is but pin money. As an indication of the sheer size of this business, in 1983 the Pentagon buying for the U.S. arsenals issued no less than fourteen million contracts to arms makers![3]

The U.S. Arms Control and Disarmament Agency calculates that in 1984 U.S. and allied arms sales and orders were in excess of 40 billion dollars. They further estimate that Soviet Bloc sales and orders were in excess of 21 billion. Without these sales, we are told, the developed nations, East and West, would no longer be able to maintain the industry, and unemployment and bankruptcy on an enormous scale would follow. However, this is another lie, the origins of which go back to the fifties and the advent of Cold War mythology when the Military-Industrial Complex, as Eisenhower christened the arms makers, rose to dominance.

In order to justify to the public and make them bear the growing burden of astronomic military spending by government which thereby continued the subsidizing of the industry, argued politicians like John Foster Dulles, it was necessary to create within the public an emotional atmosphere akin to a war-time mentality. It was necessary to create an enemy from without in order to instill fear within.

"I think there's been an illusion to some extent underlying the notion that we were always on the defensive and that the Soviet Union and the Communist Bloc was always pushing against the West. One contributing element is that the Soviet ideology itself wants to believe that it is expansive, that it is the kind of revolutionary response to the problems of the world.

"I think each leadership requires the existence of an enemy to justify this continuous mobilization of its resources and its society to pay for and be ready for major war year after year. I think one has seen in this recent period a very strong upsurge of a Cold War sentiment, partly because they wanted to acquire the resources for a great increase in defense spending and taxpayers have to be somehow led to believe that that's justifiable, and I think in the Soviet Union the inability to really satisfy minimum consumer needs has functioned in the same way as producing a requirement that the leadership finds some external enemy that is threatening Soviet survival in such a way as to justify this continued misappropriation of the resources of the country toward this kind of military weaponry.... It's waste in the most fundamental sense.... So I think that we have a kind of situation of mutual dependency between the two super powers that each...must mobilize its population around the threat posed by the other."—PROFESSOR RICHARD FALK

"In order to arm ourselves we really have to arm the world. We have to have longer production runs of equipment so that we can buy what we need, say for our Air Force or Army. We've got to produce much more of it to get it down to the price we'd like to pay. The manufacturer really has you blackmailed in that he sets the price. Then we find ourselves unable to buy enough if we don't sell even more to someone. So there's a great internal need to find market abroad."—TOM GERVASI

Rather like the TV ads and stickers that salesmen apply to the rear windows of cars which announce that they have won a major race or rally and are therefore tried and tested, the arms dealers adorn their products with an emblem which proudly proclaims "Combat Proven." There is of course no mention of the lives it cost to get that proof. For example, the Exocet missile, manufactured by Aerospatiale, a French company, gained a certain notoriety in 1982 when Margaret Thatcher felt she was putting the "Great" back in Britain by showing that she (Britain, not Mrs. Thatcher) still ruled the waves—well, a few waves surrounding a pitiful collection of rocks in the South Atlantic.

In the early afternoon of May 4, H.M.S. *Sheffield,* a destroyer in Mrs. Thatchers "Task Force" (Armada) was hit by an air-launched Exocet. Fire swept through the ship uncontrollably, frying many of her 270 crewmen. That is how the Exocet earned its "Combat Proven" award.

Barely a day before the *Sheffield* was hit, a British nuclear powered submarine, H.M.S. *Conqueror,* had torpedoed and sunk the Argentine ship *The Admiral Belgrano,* sailing alone and away from the so called "Falklands exclusion zone." Few of her 1200 crewmen survived. Needless to say, torpedoes were also stamped "Combat Proven" at Farnborough.

And once again the aim is simply to encourage the buyer to part with more and more money, whether he has any real need for the weapon or not. An Aerospatiale MM39—an Exocet to you and me—will cost you one and a half million dollars. For that you get the launch and guidance system and a missile; extra missiles are extra ("Combat Proven" stickers are thrown in for nothing). But an Exocet will not protect you from another Exocet. Oh, no. For that you need "Sea Guard" at a cost of nine million. In 1984, Sea Guard was not sporting a "Combat Proven" sticker. But it was being made and therefore had to be sold, and no doubt eventually someone, somewhere, probably in the Gulf War, will find an excuse to use it (not necessarily against an Exocet), and then Sea Guard will get its sticker.

"The production and sale of military equipment in general is not beneficial to the economy, whether that equipment goes for our own military services or for sales abroad. The reason why it is sold abroad is to bring down the prices to our own services as I mentioned. The problem with the production of military equipment is that it is not equipment that gets into the economy and is used—thank the lord, for as much as it isn't used, we should be grateful. What it does instead is simply sit there, and so the productive capacity of a society is being diverted; resources, sometimes quite scarce and irretrievable resources, are being used to make all these things which don't go back into the economy. The Congressional Budget Office did a study showing what would happen if the billions of dollars that is spent on weapons were spent on something else. They found that every ten billion would create forty thousand more jobs than ten billion invested in weapons, and that is an enormously important thing for people to remember. We hear constantly the argument that, "Well, this is wonderful for society and the economy because it produces jobs." It does not....

"In the past four years of the Reagan administration's rule the country has spent more than a trillion dollars....This is now 26 percent of the federal budget. It is something like 9 percent of our gross national product, whereas in Japan it is 2 percent, which is one of the reasons why the Japanese are so productive because they're making more and better civilian goods and services and their economy is benefitting from it because it all is used."—TOM GERVASI

Militarism and the arms race are leaching the developed nations as they destroy people and economies in the developing world. Men, materials and money are consumed in ever greater quantities to the detriment of the majority.

- Twenty percent of the world's scientists are involved in weapons research.[4]
- Twenty-five percent of all research and development world-wide is swallowed up by military programs.[5]
- Fifty percent of all British Government research and development goes on weapons.[6]
- Between 1981 and '84 the Reagan administration gained congressional approval for $889 billion for military spending. This represented a staggering 97.5 percent of all the dollars that it asked Congress to approve.[7]
- More financial and intellectual resources are allocated to weapons world-wide than research on health, food production, energy and environmental protection.[8]
- In 1985 the world spent $910 billion for arms and the military but during the same period the World Health Organization had a total budget of only $520 million. That is equivalent to just six hours of military spending.[9]

"When a weapons system is sold to a country, particularly a country that doesn't have a lot of money, it can have a very detrimental effect, because if the country does not have any other way of raising the price to pay for it it must borrow the money, and who does it borrow the money from—the United States. And our banks are prepared to lend money at very favorable interest rates and these loans are often guaranteed because they're done by an export/import bank in Washington which has the enormous, the extraordinary prerogative of guaranteeing the loans at the taxpayers' expense. In other words, if a debtor nation should fail to pay, the U.S. taxpayer would come in and bale them out."—TOM GERVASI

Once we have decided that we can open up an area for sales, even if the government there is not particularly favorable to us, it becomes a kind of an addiction, a vicious spiral, which requires greater and greater investment and co-operation from that government. They need more and more of it, and it's so expensive they can't pay for it, so they must borrow—and they borrow from us. In order to repay us, all they see…is more of their wealth going out of the country and coming to us, and that won't pay anything more than the interest on the debt they already owe; so it's a continuing involvement and gets deeper and deeper, just as it does when an addict has to get heavier and heavier into his dependence on heroin.

> Since that is the momentum we already have built our system on, obviously we need Third World wars. The developed nations think they need to sell weapons since that is what they have been doing. Their defense industries know no other model to follow but growth. So they will grow and continue to produce tanks, whether tanks are any longer what we need or anyone else needs, and unfortunately in the Third World there is as you know a variety…of conflicts—regional, national, tribal, familial—and when people have weapons they tend to use them. That's the problem. We don't want them used and they sit idle on our tarmacs and so forth, but there are many areas of the world where people do actually have a demand—another demand we create. They're out there looking because they are at war or will be if they can manage to buy the weapons. We have supplied India and Pakistan in this way. They've fought each other a couple of times with the same equipment supplied by the same supplier. We've seen this in the Middle East numerous times. I don't know how many times Israeli tanks made in Detroit have faced Jordanian and Syrian tanks made in Detroit and Egyptian tanks made in Detroit. Obviously if we are producing things that we do not need and cannot even justify to our people, although the Reagan administration has probably outdone any government in history at making such a justification, then we're going to be supplying them abroad, and when that happens we are fueling wars."—TOM GERVASI

From Iran and Iraq, who collectively spend over a billion and a half oil dollars a month pursuing their war and purchasing weapons and munitions to kill each other,[10] through Africa Asia and the Americas, the developed nations fuel wars and perpetuate the system without conscience. There exists two moralities. The one which our governments tell us they hold to and the other they actually practice. Publicly they profess to hold high-sounding ideals for the promotion of democracy, freedom and independence. Privately they believe that they must sell the technology of death to regimes which in most cases abjure democracy and freedom but with whom there is an exploitative relationship which the super powers consider beneficial. For how many years did the U.S. and its allies shore up Batista and Somoza, Marcos, the Duvaliers and Haile Selassie? For how many more will they be blind to Pinochet and Chun Doo Hwan of South Korea or the Salvadoran oligarchy and their Death Squads or King Hassan of Morocco, the largest recipient of U.S. military assistance after Israel? How many more Hungaries and Czechoslovakias, Polands and Afghanistans must there be?

ERITREA
"A stupid way of doing business"

In the Horn of Africa the Ethiopean army, which suppresses internal freedoms while attempting to smash the Eritrean's struggle for independence, is now three hundred thousand strong—and armies of this size are always hungry for weapons.

"It is now estimated in fact that some $3.5 to $4 billion worth of arms has been already transferred to Ethiopia by the Soviet Union and it will continue because a lot of it has been lost in battles in Eritrea, and the Ethiopian army is now the largest army in sub-Sahara Africa, which means more weapons, more arms.... It's been a disaster. I don't think Ethiopia has started paying its debt yet, I don't see how it can. So that future generations' fortune is ransomed on this war. The effect of the war and the militarization of Ethiopian society as a whole has been devastating on Ethiopia's productive capacity. The food shortage is there because able-bodied people are forced to leave their peaceful productive activities to fight in wars they do not support or understand."—BEREKET SELASSIE, Professor of International Law

"Famine follows war, generally speaking. Obviously, war isn't the only cause but it would be very simple-minded to look at famine, for instance in Africa, and say, 'Well, this is simply a result of the rains failing, or simply a result of misguided development policies.' It's so often forgotten how many wars are going on in the Third World, and it's forgotten that these must be having an effect and are having an effect...and famine is one of the most obvious ones. If you just look at the refugee situation, you have millions and millions of refugees around the world who've been driven out of their homes and away from their crops. In an agricultural economy, once you've left your home then you have no way of feeding yourself, or maintaining yourself. So war doesn't just destroy food, it also drives people away, or in the conscription system, of course, forcibly extracts a lot of the people from the system. And really, the links between war and the effects of war, namely famine, just have not been properly drawn and...the sad thing about the Ethiopian situation is that that enormous response, particularly in Britain, to seeing the effects of starvation, just has not been channeled into a proper understanding of the politics and the background."—BARBARA ROGERS, former consultant to U.N.D.P. and F.A.O.

"It's a bankrupt government right now. It's the West that really holds that government together economically, while the Soviet Union holds it together militarily. I have interviewed Ethiopean prisoners of war who talk about having been paid often in food, rather than in money. I have gone into captured Ethiopian garrisons and seen great food stocks marked clearly, 'For free distribution only.' 'Gift of the E.E.C.' and so on, stocked up in these garrisons to feed the army."—DAN CONNELL, Grass Roots International

"*Where have you come from and how long did it take you and your children to get here?*"

"She is saying, she come from Habilla Logho, it takes for walking four days."

"*Her daughter appears to have glaucoma of the right eye, can she see with it?*"

"She says she does not know what it is called but this girl only she can see a bit."

"*Has a doctor examined her?...Why does she laugh at that?*"

"She says she is a peasant, she does not know a doctor. Many of the children have this in the eyes but what can they do....You know she ask can you look at it, you see she thinks because you are white you are a doctor...they don't see many white people anymore, the children almost never they have seen."

"*Why did she have to leave Habilla Logho?*"

"There they don't have food. The Derg do not give to them food, the army has it. For three years now they only have little food."

"*Ibrahim, would you please ask the little girl how long it is since she had an egg or milk?*"

"She does not understand you...."

"*Why?*"

"It is so long now, she is only seven, and they have not these things, milk, for two, three years. She does not know what you are talking about."—
IBRAHIM SAID (ERA), translating for MILETA MESFIN and her children

"From whom did he buy this milk powder?"

"He is saying that the army sells it and then he buy it from certain small merchants."

"So the Ethiopean Army sells it to small merchants, then these merchants here in Eritrea buy it from them...?"

"Yes, they buy it from Karen and bring here to Germika."

"And where will he take it from here?"

"They take it to Kassala, Sudan."

"So he is taking food that was given by the European Economic Community for Ethiopia, which he bought, through Eritrea, where people are starving, into Sudan?"

"Yes, that is right."—Te'ame, E.P.L.F. Interpreter

E.R.A., Eritrea's own relief association, does everything it can to alleviate the suffering caused by both the famine and the war but they have few resources and even less funds, for not only are the Eritreans unsupported militarily by any outside source, they also remain outcast by the majority of governmental aid agencies. By the time the milk powder reaches Germika its price is so inflated that E.R.A. cannot afford to buy it from the traders, so it and other stolen relief goods travel the last few miles from Germika to Kassala, just across the Sudanese border. At the same time, thousands of starving Eritreans fleeing the constant bombardment of the Soviet Migs have had to make the same journey in search of food.

For many the end of the line is the refugee camp at Wad Sharifeh, a searing patch of desert just inside Sudan. By January 1985 the camp's population had grown in just three months from 3,000 to 49,000. With no shade and in temperatures in excess of 120 degrees, they slowly died in tents made of rags and dried leaves, and there was just one well to serve everyone.

"One well for forty-nine thousand people. It's nothing. It's nothing. We could put a roof over the whole camp and it could all be one hospital, it's that bad. When we first opened the pediatric center we were taking every child who was sick and a lot of them were dying, and much as we tried to help it was impossible. Now we only accept those that we think have a chance to live. The severely ill children, the ones that are dying, they have to go back to their hut to die."

"About a week before Christmas an air lift was announced. Did that arrive?"

"Here in Kassala we got two or three planeloads of goods. Some were tents, some were blankets, there was a little bit of food. But really it's nothing for all these people."

"Do these people need tents and blankets now?"

"Number one need is water, and the second need is food."

"Why is there no food? Who is responsible for giving food to this camp?"

"Myself, I don't understand. We're under the umbrella of UNHCR. Our food was coming from the World Food Program, but I hear there is just no food in this country."

"So it's just not getting through to Sudan?"

"There's no food in Sudan as far as I know."—DIANE MACKEE, Canadian Red Cross

On January 20, 1985, the first logistics team from the World Food Program arrived at Wad Sharifeh to "assess the situation." Diane Mackee gave it to them straight from the shoulder, leaving them in no doubt as to how she viewed the professed humanitarian concern of the international community. When approached, not surprisingly, they were unwilling to explain to me why it had taken them three months to come to Wad Sharifeh and were even less inclined to tell me why there was no food there. Eventually a Scandinavian member of the team said, "We are just the officers, the employees of the WFP. We are at the mercy of donor governments. If they don't want, for their own political reasons, to send food, then we are powerless. This is a very political situation, the emphasis is on Ethiopia, not these refugees from Eritrea and Tigre.... This is of course off the record...." Sorry but when peoples lives are being ruined, nothing is off the record.

The people at Wad Sharifeh are the end result of decisions taken thousands of miles away by men and women who have no concern for the consequences of their actions as the super powers play geo-politics over the Horn of Africa. Without the war and with realistic development programs which were and are possible, none of them would be dying.

From Moscow, which provides the arms, to Whitehall and Washington, who had to be shamed into providing food, by rock stars and ordinary people, the Eritrean people matter little as both power blocs woo the Ethiopian government for their own perceived strategic gain.

> "I don't hold out a great deal of hope for this child. She's less than 60 percent of the normal weight, and below 60 percent they have very little chance of survival. Oh, it's heartbreaking to see the children die, especially as you get to know them. And really when you think the main problem is the food in this camp. It makes me very angry, because there's food in the world, there's just none in Sudan right now.
>
> *"When you talk to the people, why do they say that they're coming here to Kassala?"*
>
> "They give two reasons. They're coming because of the fighting inside their own country, and also because of the drought."
>
> *"But these are people that are coming from areas that are supposed to be controlled by the Ethiopian government. Do they say there's any food where they are, where they've come from?"*
>
> "I don't think there's very much food at all inside Eritrea."
>
> *"Even in spite of the fact that the world's attention has been on Ethiopia and food is supposed to be pouring in?"*
>
> "This is the northern part, and the government is stopping the food from getting in, from what I understand."—DIANE MACKEE

The village of Habilla Shillalo in southern Eritrea has become a way-station for Eritreans and Tigreans searching for food. Many of the original inhabitants have taken the journey to Wad Sharifeh, few have returned. Habilla Shillalo hasn't changed much in the past couple of hundred years. It sits on parched red earth, picking its way over rocks and boulders which also form most of the thatched-roofed huts. On the slope at the edge of the village is the camel-driven oil mill where the blinkered animal endlessly describes the same circle that its ancestors have worn over the centuries. The air is a

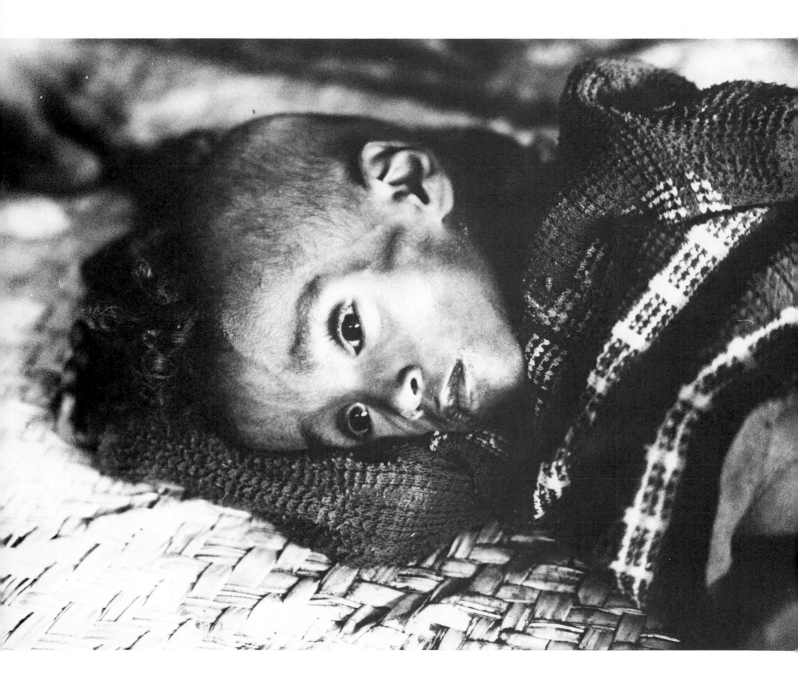

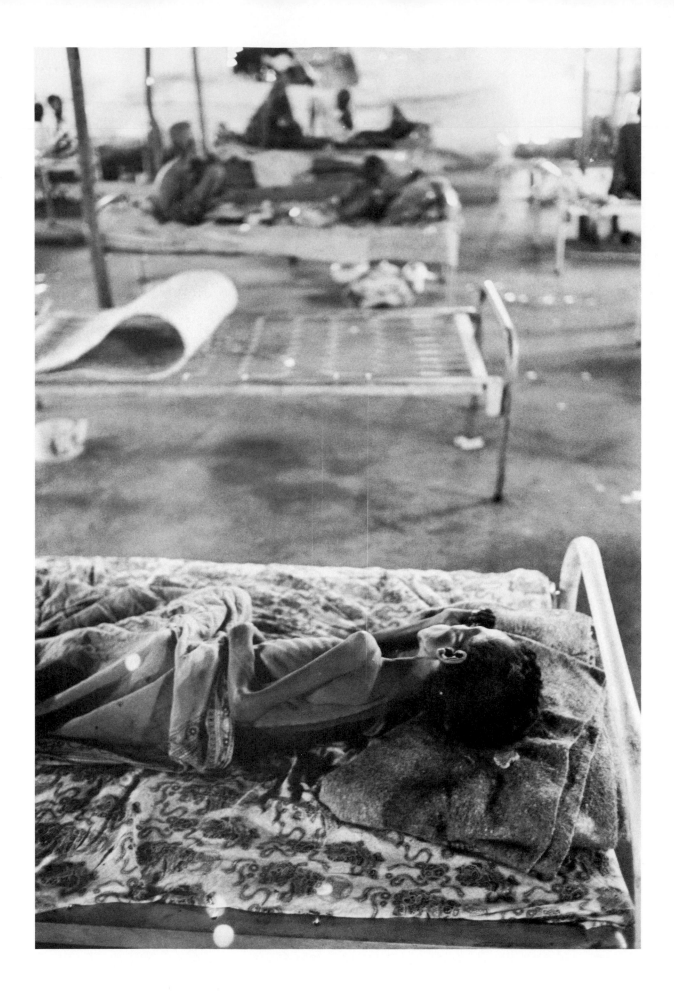

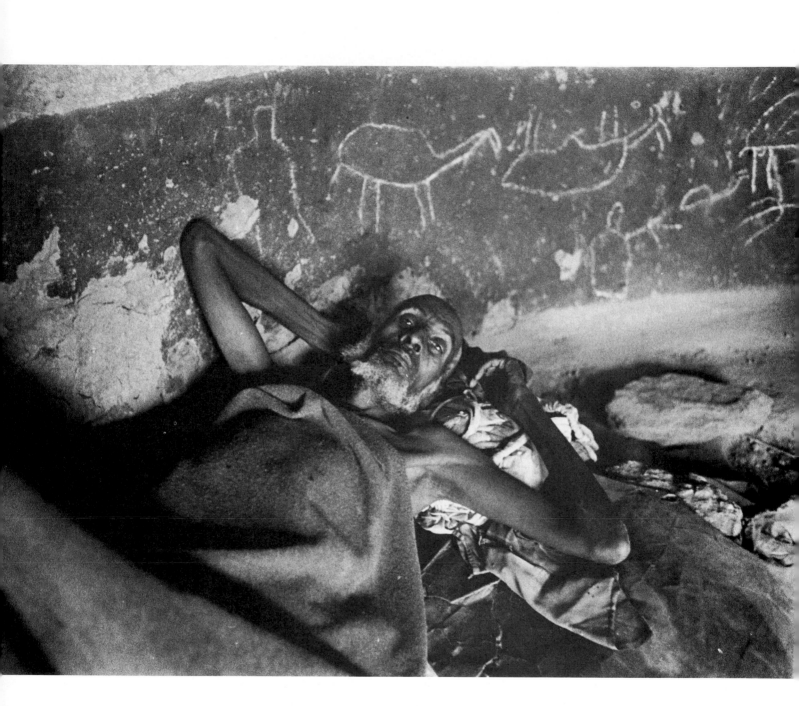

clouded veil, thick with dust and flies, which hangs over everything. People seem to just sit, all day long. Not because they can't do anything, but because there is nothing to do. It has not rained here for three years. It is so dry that it is impossible to believe that there was ever water here. You cannot imagine this brick and ochre-colored land was ever green. But it was, once; before the drought, and before the war.

There is water, but it is a mile away—a well cut deep into the bedrock—which is all there is to serve the populations of this and another village. Wells like this could be put in all over the country, if only the bombing would stop. If only the war would end, development projects, like water and irrigation systems, would be simple and cheap to achieve to help the Eritreans rebuild for themselves. If only the war would end those projects would cost less than the cost of the war and the emergency feeding. If only the war would stop, Eritreans would be able to live in peace and without pain and it would cost everyone less. But the war hasn't stopped since 1962. The land won't support anything and they have no seed anyway. The villagers of Habilla Shillalo and places like it rely almost exclusively on E.R.A., who are shunned internationally because they don't fit in politically to the wider scheme.... If only the war would end.

"It's politics clearly and simply that is killing the Eritrean people. You have about 95 percent of the aid coming into this region going through government channels, and perhaps 5 percent of that coming into Eritrea, equivalent to what the Eritrean Relief Association counts as 5 percent of its need. The people are, in many cases, only one or two hours' drive from the Sudan border. There is no problem with getting the food from one place to the other, but neither governments nor private agencies want to invest in that operation, despite knowing that the need is there. Since the late 1970's, when the Soviet Union came in here, the U.S. strategy has been geared toward displacing the Soviet Union, often not so much for a positive interest in Ethiopia, as it were, but a negative interest in getting rid of the Soviet Union. The Ethiopian government is constantly saying that they have access to all the areas where there are people in need. I have met government officials, the chairperson of the Relief and Rehabilitation Commission, seen him sit in a meeting with U.S. AID officials and say exactly the same thing, when all of us there [not only myself] but all the other aid agencies which were operating under government auspices in Ethiopia, know it not to be true because they themselves are not permitted often even into the government-held towns, let alone the rural areas. The problem is that knowing that, they remain quiet about it. The United Nations, for example, UNICEF, in September of 1984 put out a report that there were 6 million people in urgent need in northern Ethiopia, but only 1 million were reachable, implying that the others were perhaps in remote mountain areas, but nothing about the war.... The drought is only part of the problem. War is the other part. There have to be international moves for a ceasefire in Eritrea to allow the food to move in."—DAN CONNELL

"This drought situation and famine has become a political weapon in itself. It's being used as a card for winning back the Derg, not for giving humanitarian aid to the needy civilian population. It's a game of the big powers and I think the population has got nothing to do with such policies

"You would presumably offer safe passage to any food aid coming into this country?"

"Well, I think it would be very naïve not to accept that. In the first place, it's to the benefit of the civilian population and that would do no harm to anybody in Eritrea; a safe pass to areas even under the control of the Derg."

"Do the Derg allow safe passage of food into Eritrea?"

"I think that would never be dreamt of."

"Your food convoys travel at night. Why is that?"

"You have their Migs flying every day to see that we never use our transport resources to give relief aid to the civilian population."

"Have they tried to attack the food convoys?"

"I think that has been an everyday experience everywhere."—ISAIAS AFEWORKI, Vice Secretary General, E.P.L.F.

Since the begining Eritrea has been appealing for a U.N. referendum to decide the future and end the war. Neither Haile Selassie nor the Derg nor the international community have responded to those appeals. Similarly Isaias Afeworki's offer for a ceasefire was ignored and, consequently, Eritreans, Tigreans and Ethiopians continued to die almost unnoticed.[1]

"Of course, the famine in Africa really wasn't news until the television footage of people dying in Ethiopia, two years at least after the beginning of the problem surfaced to many who were on the scene. But television in effect creates the story now, and the print media have to follow that. Without a television picture or something visual, it's as if it doesn't exist. We had the opportunity to act in Eritrea in 1983 to prevent the famine that we see today. All the information was there. We even had one American TV network come in and film situations in Eritrea. That film was not broadcast, because there were simply not enough bodies piling up to make it a spectacular story. All you had was malnutrition and the forecast of famine coming. Forecasts aren't stories...."—DAN CONNELL

On January 9 Isaac Anenya, a native of Habilla Shillalo was still able to get around. He was a Coptic Christian and this was the Coptic Christmas period, a time for reflection. Once he had been a moderately successful farmer by local standards, but now at nearly sixty he had nothing. Malnutrition and accompanying disease were killing both Isaac and his family. His once-strong body was so weak that he couldn't even pick up a rock the size of a grapefruit.

The following day he could no longer walk and was having difficulty breathing. "What can I do" he whispered, "I'm just waiting to die." By sunrise he was dead.

His wife and family passed the next seven days just sitting outside their

home in mourning. They didn't even raise their eyes when the Ethiopian Migs made their daily swoop over the village.

"Ethiopia is a classic case. You have external forces involving governments, voluntary agencies and all kinds of money, we don't know where it comes from. Now, in fact, it might be a lot better for everybody just to get out of there and let the Ethiopians settle the situation for themselves, and if the result is a government we don't particularly like, that's too bad. Because the result of this constant intervention, and in some cases an external agency switching wildly from one side to the other, as the Americans have done in Ethiopia and in the whole horn of Africa, is the dislocation and the continuation of war over, in this case, many decades....And I don't see how you can see the situation in Ethiopia and that region, and look at the starvation, and not take into account the decades of war that have been going on."—BARBARA ROGERS

MOZAMBIQUE

"Strategic Interests"

But it isn't just Ethiopia. Ignored by the spotlight of television and the press, at least seven other African countries are suffering the plagues of famine and war. In Mozambique food trucks can only move with military escorts to protect them from rebels known as the M.N.R. Like the Contras in Nicaragua, the M.N.R., or RENAMO as they are also known, have no real political motivation, and in fact are just another proxy army, their pay-masters being the South African Government who wish to make life unbearable for Mozambicans and FRELIMO, their socialist government.

During the war of independence to end illegal white minority rule in neighboring Rhodesia, Ken Flowers, Ian Smith's head of the Rhodesian Central Intelligence Organization, decided to set up a private army, a kind of fifth column, which would operate from within Mozambique and be composed mainly of Mozambicans. In 1974 Mozambique, a former Portuguese colony, was all but independent after ten years of ruinous and merciless war, and Mozambicans who had been part of PIDE, the colonial secret police (which like the Guardia Nacional in Nicaragua had served their masters' whims in the years of blood-letting), fled to Rhodesia, fearing post-independence vengeance. These men together with members of the elite and hated G.E.P. paratroop force, whom the Portuguese had also formed, were recruited by Flowers for two specific tasks. Firstly they were to attack Mozambican based units of Robert Mugabe's liberation army, and secondly, since independent black states were anathema to Flowers and Ian Smith, this private army was to begin a process of armed destabilization of FRELIMO.

South Africa does not like black independent states on her doorstep either, for the same reason that the U.S. has no love of independent states in Central America—if they are successful they might be an example to others, and that would never do—so when Zimbabwe finally won her independence in 1980 and Flowers could no longer pay the M.N.R., Pretoria took over these bandits, paying them to attack vital economic and strategic installations and increase the internal pressure on FRELIMO.

Of course, it is not Pretoria's intention that the M.N.R. should win and become a government (the M.N.R. is capable of neither anyway), but simply that they make life and post independence development impossible. Furthermore, the situation has the tacit approval of certain western governments because FRELIMO has an ever-growing military and economic relationship with the Soviet Union, which has her own motives for being there. So hurting Mozambique hurts Moscow. And that in the end is the name of the game.

From 1980 onwards the South African government poured money into the M.N.R. providing equipment, training and logistical support to bandits operating from bases both in South Africa and within Mozambique itself. As the war intensified whole provinces were cut off from Maputo, the capital; roads and tracks were mined and travelers ambushed. The vital rail link from the oil port of Beira, on which land-locked Zimbabwe depends, was cut, as was the line which comes from Zambia and runs through Tete province to the coast. Vast stocks of coal, normally a lucrative export, built up at the pit heads in Tete because the trains couldn't run. At the same time South Africa cut back 75 percent of her use of the port of Maputo, thereby reducing Mozambique's foreign earnings (though Pretoria must have instructed the M.N.R. not to touch the rail line that comes from South Africa because it is still carrying South African coal for export through Maputo, which is a cheaper route than using her own Port Elizabeth).

In the two years 1982/83, the M.N.R. destroyed 840 schools, 212 health posts, a minimum of 200 villages and over 900 shops. Through those two years the war in all of its forms cost Mozambique over eighteen hundred million dollars.[1] All of this, combined with the effects of economic sabotage by the departing Portuguese colonists, forced Mozambique in effect to declare bankruptcy in 1984 by asking to reschedule payment of her foreign debts, which were then in excess of $1.4 billion, saying that she would not be able to service the interest of $714 million until 1990.[2]

Then came the drought that has hit so many countries in sub-Saharan Africa and in early 1984 a cyclone that destroyed roads and powerlines and swept away vital top soil. Mozambique was on its knees; the elements and destabilization were working.

It would have been impractical and not politically expedient to turn to Moscow for combat troops, and economic help was being denied her by COMECON. Finally, with no other alternative, Mozambique was forced to sign the Nkomati agreement of March 1984 with South Africa. On the surface it might seem fine to make a "non-aggression" pact with so powerful a neighbor, the terms of which were that South Africa would end her control and support of the M.N.R. and in exchange Mozambique should expel members of the A.N.C. (the African National Congress that is fighting to abolish apartheid in South Africa and is to Black South Africans what the P.L.O. is to Palestinians). However, for a front-line state to sign any agreement with Pretoria is nothing short of defeat, and of course while Mozambique did, with great pain, expel the A.N.C., South Africa continued active support and direction of the M.N.R.

All of this increased Mozambique's military dependence on Moscow, with more and more Soviet Military advisers coming in to help run the war and thereby giving Moscow the chance to exert some influence over access to Mozambican resources.

By 1984/5 the famine had really taken hold and M.N.R. attacks made the task of getting food through to the starving at times almost impossible.

Though the details may be different from the Horn of Africa, the overall problem remains the same. The will of the so-called "free world" to put pressure on Pretoria to end the war and help feed Mozambicans is not conditioned by their need but by "geo-political interests."

"Do you have the milk powder, the maize, etc., that you need?"

"No we have nothing. They get a government supply of maize meal but they actually need things like milk, milk powder and general high protein foods...they have nothing, they have nothing..."

"Have you asked for that or has the camp asked for that?"

"The government is doing its best but the enormity of the need is the problem. Even if the medical supplies and food are brought into the area, getting it to the people is a major problem."

"How much are the efforts of the government and people like yourselves being hampered by the war, by the existence of the M.N.R.?"

"They have attacked this camp more than once in the past month. Most of their banditry is geared towards taking food and just terrorizing the population.

"But the M.N.R. claim that they are representing the population of Mozambique, that the population supports them."

"When someone holds a gun to your head I don't think you have much political choice. It's a matter of survival."—REV. LLOYD THOMAS and NURSE GILLIAN WRIGHT, Volunteer Aid Workers from South African Baptist Church

There is a ward in the Maputo General Hospital that is entirely full of women lacking one or both breasts and men with no noses. These are not victims of a medically diagnosible cancer, but a cancer none the less—the M.N.R. Each one of these people has been "taught a lesson" by those brave agents of South Africa, for daring to support FRELIMO. They are not unique. Throughout the country, the M.N.R. butcher civilians on a daily basis while continuing to claim that they are trying to liberate Mozambique.

"People who cut breasts and noses and ears and put landmines in places where they know only civilians can move, it's very difficult for me to understand that people like that can make propaganda, that they are making a struggle for the people, for the freedom of the people and so on. When they go into a communal village with one thousand people, two, three hundred families, and they put fire in all the communal village, they are not creating problems to the government, to FRELIMO, they are creating problems to the people, because the houses belong to the people not to the government. And they take two, three, four months to build a house and they go there and put fire. And you can find places in Mozambique where they have put fire four times in the same communal village, you can find these places, for instance in Manica."—Dr. Evo Garrido, Maputo General Hospital

Mozambique is a large country and communications between Maputo and the northern provinces are bad at the best of times. But with the M.N.R. constantly cutting the roads, nothing can move. People can't trade; kids can't go to school, so the future is also being ransomed. In countries like this—Nicaragua or Vietnam, for example—either at war or living with the legacy, it is easy as a foreigner to be overwhelmed by the situation, to be taken over by the statistics and the politics, to be so concerned with the overall issues that one misses, if one is not careful, the minutiae. But it is the little things that really show what the situation means to ordinary people. For example, the first words that a foreigner will hear from a Mozambican are, "Have you got any soap?"

In the once-rich Portuguese resort town of Beira they have no electricity, no water, little food and no beer. The Hotel Don Carlos, in the past a favorite with the colonials, can offer you a bed, but nothing else, and in the center of town even the "Dollar Shop"—that Alladin's cave where foreigners and well-to-do Mozambicans alike can normally spend their greenbacks on imported goods, foodstuffs and ice-cold canned beer—is closed because the shelves are bare.

There are trucks here to transport food to the interior of the province, but since the oil terminal in the docks was hit by the M.N.R. there is no fuel for them, and anyway the roads into the interior are mined.

"The people is suffering from hunger and from war at the same time. You cannot do anything to develop Mozambique if you don't stop the war. If you try to put in a pump, they come and destroy the pump. If you try to build a house, they come and destroy the house. If you try to make some crops, they put fire on the crops. If you send a motor car with something to the people, they stop the car, they destroy the car. It's impossible. First of all you must stop the war. We must have peace."—DR. EVO GARRIDO

Development is the key word, but development might just help the Mozambicans towards real independence.

"I've been here seven months as a "fire-fighter" for CARE. There is nothing here. Even if you have money it buys you nothing.... There has been one train from Beira to Tete with food in seven months. There's nothing in the shops.... The agencies and their governments are to blame. CARE is 90 percent funded by the State Department, we are an arm of American foreign policy.... If we asked for $20 million for Mozambique we would get it, for the emergency, 'cause the U.S. were out, now we are in. We are the pathfinders for U.S. capital in these countries. But there are no pens or pencils in the schools in my area, I can't get them 'cause my budget is not for education. CARE's administration budget here is $2.5 million. I could buy literally thousands of pens and paper, but that would be development, not an emergency need, and is therefore forbidden.... I was eight years in Chad, but it wasn't as bad as this. I don't care if I am fired for saying this. We should be doing more. There are good people here, perhaps the best both at the top and at the bottom. They don't deserve what they are getting."
—CARE Field Worker

The security situation in some provinces is so bad that the only way to get relief to the starving is with an aging DC-3. The irony is that while South Africa pays the M.N.R.. to wage war in Mozambique, the Mozambican Red Cross has to pay a South African company for the use of the plane.

"Well, when we were there in August of 1983, it was quite clear that South Africa in fact was engaged in all-out war against the Front-Line nations and it was using a variety of actions to destabilize the governments of those countries, either to keep them off-keel or make them so vulnerable economically that they would in fact enter into negotiated agreements with South Africa. And South Africa points to those agreements as an indication that, in fact, it does too get along with its neighbors: 'Look at the agreements we are able to negotiate with them." —CONGRESSMAN TED WEISS

"The Nkomati agreement was a series of undertakings in which the Mozambicans agreed that they would not serve as a springboard for A.N.C.

activity directed against South Africa, and South Africans in a reciprocal manner undertook not to become involved in serving as a springboard for M.N.R. activity into Mozambique. It is our general impression that both sides have lived up to their commitments in that regard. The fact that the war inside Mozambique has not come to an end, that there is no ceasefire, is of great concern to us and as long as that situation continues will be of great concern to us, because clearly one of the fruits of the Nkomati process was to bring about stability and peace and development for Mozambique, but I think it would be going well beyond that facts to argue that the reason that that war continues is...as simple as your question implies...that cross border supply of the M.N.R. by South Africa hasn't ceased."—DR. CHESTER CROCKER. U.S. Assistant Secretary of State:Africa

"The Mozambicans in fact adhered to the commitments that they made. The South Africans, for whatever reason, have not been able to implement their side of the bargain and there can be an argument as to whether it's in fact the government of South Africa or whether it's the military within South Africa, whether it's the Portuguese nationalists who are calling the shots either in Portugal or in South Africa. The fact is that Mozambique did not get what it bargained for and the United States again has been of the opinion that working behind the scenes it could be more effective with South Africa than publicly condemning it."—CONGRESSMAN TED WEISS

"No doubt there's been private trafficking and so forth, but I don't think that the South African armed forces are likely to violate the stated policy of the State President of South Africa, which is that this activity was supposed to cease as of the signing of the Nkomati agreement."

"I accept that it was supposed to cease. What is however quite apparent is that there is still cross-border supplying of the M.N.R. by the South African military, that there is contact on a daily basis between South African military personnel and the M.N.R. I know that South African military officers have entered Mozambican territory since Nkomati—I've seen photographs of them shown to me by the M.N.R. I can't believe that the Intelligence Services of the United States—which is far more sophisticated in its information gathering techniques than I am—don't have similar information."

"Well, you may have information that is not available to me. I don't have such information. My...information would indicate that having helped to create the M.N.R. into the rebel force that it is, the South African government has found it rather difficult...to bring about a pattern of control over its activities such that you'd see an actual ceasefire develop. We do not have information that would confirm your statement that the South African military is continuing to supply the Mozambique resistance."—DR. CHESTER CROCKER

Dr. Crocker is the architect of the Reagan administration's policy towards South Africa known as "Constructive Engagement," another fine piece of official newspeak. Constructive engagement means that rather than the imposition of effective sanctions or actual condemnation of Apartheid, the White House believes that it can change the political course of events in southern Africa by on-going "dialogue." So periodically Dr. Crocker visits Pretoria and informs the South African Government that the President and the people of the United States want to see an end to apartheid and the South Africans are polite but obstinate, and then Dr. Crocker goes away again. This policy ignores the fact that Pretoria has no intention of anything other than cosmetic change and that, since the implementation of constructive engagement, violence and repression have increased. In effect, constructive engagement has been taken as a signal by Pretoria that they have carte blanche to do whatever they like to their own Black dis-enfranchized majority and to their Black neighbors.

It continues to be a constant source of amazement to me that diplomats and politicians lie blatantly, and at times unnecessarily, particularly to the media, when they know— as Dr. Crocker must have when he said, "We do not have information that would confirm your statement that the South African military is continuing to supply the Mozambique resistance"—the lie is so transparent. Perhaps they feel that this is a necessary part of the game of deceit that officialdom plays with the public. Perhaps if Dr. Crocker admitted that he knew of the on-going support of the M.N.R. by South Africa he would feel that he was compromising the U.S. relationship with Pretoria, a relationship that is motivated by balance sheets. If that is the case, compromising the lives of ordinary Mozambicans is probably of only passing concern. If on the other hand Dr. Crocker was not lying, then the C.I.A. Station Chief for the area ought to be hauled over the coals for not being able to furnish the Assistant Secretary of State with information that was available to me and as a shaper of U.S. foreign policy he should have had.

Whatever reasons Dr. Crocker may have had for his denial, the South African government admitted their continuing and active involvement with the M.N.R. in September 1985.

Though the long-term goals for Mozambique of South Africa and the West may differ slightly, they remain fundamentally the same and to those ends they work together towards the subjugation of FRELIMO and the easing out of the Soviet Union. In 1981, South African commandos bombed a suburb of Maputo, purportedly acting on intelligence supplied to them by the C.I.A.[3]

"After the Matola raid in January 1981, Mozambique exposed a C.I.A. network in Mozambique and expelled quite a few C.I.A. agents who were working in the American embassy. The American ambassador left at that time, and the Americans just wouldn't give any aid for something like two, three years until round about the time of the Nkomati Accord. There was a visit from a U.S. AID man and the situation improved. But for three years, the country that probably gives more aid than any other in the world just decided not to give any to Mozambique."—DEREK PARDEY, Development Agency Field Officer, Maputo

During that three years probably one hundred thousand Mozambicans died of starvation.[4] But what was the Soviet Union doing if the States would not help? The answer is precious little. They have introduced teachers and doctors and geologists, but have trained few Mozambicans in these much-needed professions and have declared that they cannot support FRELIMO because it professes to be only Marxist oriented and not a full Marxist-Leninist party.[5] If that is the criterion then Moscow should put its own house in order. Marx and Lenin would turn in their graves if they knew what system obtained in Soviet Russia in their names. Finally, they have refused Mozambique access to COMECON financial support on the grounds that they are economically unstable. They don't apply the same rules to Vietnam or Cuba, but then, unlike Vietnam and Cuba, Mozambique has declared that no foreign power, West or East, shall have military bases on her soil, and so far Moscow has not been able to turn the screw hard enough to force Mozambique to change this policy. So lacking rights to have bases in Mozambique, Moscow does not perceive any great immediate strategic gain, but being there is better than not—it keeps the door open and annoys the West. Therefore, until such time as she can exert enough pressure to gain even limited base facilities, she will simply continue to send advisors to help run the war and supply weapons to fight it; any other help will not be forthcoming.[6]

> "I think there's political motivation to aid going into any country. I don't think it would be specific to Mozambique. I mean I think it was President Nixon, one of the relatively recent American Presidents, who said quite blatantly that foreign aid was an arm of American Foreign Policy and make no bones about it."—DEREK PARDEY

* * *

The use of aid as a weapon is by no means restricted to food and emergency supplies. In 1983 the Nicaraguan government applied to the Inter-American Development Bank, a section of the World Bank, for a loan to help build up a fishing fleet near the port of Corinto. The Bank, which is supposed to be non-political when making its decisions, agreed to the loan, but the U.S. representative, acting on instructions which are believed to have come from the State Department, insisted that an extraordinary clause be added to the agreement in which Nicaragua had to be able to guarantee that adequate

supplies of fuel would be available to run the fleet. The clause was unique; nothing like it had been included in previous agreements. However, since Corinto was one of the country's main oil terminals, Managua saw no problem in accepting it. The fishing boats would be a valuable boost to the local economy, which was already suffering as a result of the U.S.-instigated Contra war. But within just a few weeks, the special clause took on a new significance.

"Well it came at night, about eleven-thirty at night. The attack began with a Piranha Motor launch firing at the tanks. It got into the bay and started bombarding. A launch supported by a plane, which was trying to divert our attention. When there is an air attack we don't expect an attack from a boat and so we centered our attention on the plane, and that allowed them to…"

"How much of the installation was lost?"

"Well, you can count them. We had that one there, two, three, that one too is practically useless also. Four tanks and those over there had to be repaired. We also lost other fuel."

"How much is it going to cost to replace?"

"About five million…dollars. Five million dollars."—RAMON F.S.L.N. Representative, Corinto

The attack, which was clearly designed to make it impossible for Nicaragua to honor its guarantee to maintain adequate fuel supplies, was in fact directed by the C.I.A.[1]

But the super powers are by no means alone in their manipulation of important development aid sources. In line with the British commitment to adhere to U.S. policy towards Nicaragua a confidential Foreign Office instruction by a Mr. J.W. Watt entitled "Voting Policy at the I.A.D.B. and I.B.R.D.," dated October, 12, 1984, states in reference to Nicaragua:

> There is no need to amend our voting policy towards Nicaragua for the time being. The problem of explaining it in public will, however, persist and we shall need to stick to our present line *of claiming that our opposition is based on technical grounds.*[2] *(Emphasis added.)*

A British government official who received the document noted in the margin, "if we can find them!"

"We always hear about our strategic or security interests, but in fact I think they're chiefly an excuse for the economic interests. Sometimes there is a reason to say, 'We must keep open...the sea channels,' as they put it, 'we must preserve our right of passage'—passage to where? To what? To those resources that we want; and the strategic argument, as it is otherwise construed, is mostly hogwash, isn't it. It's meant to say that, 'Unless we have favorable governments we cannot do trade; we will lose our wealth.' It's construed as a problem of '..unfavorable governments that will not be compatible with us.' Now where is the proof of that? Many countries want good relations with us and do not wish to suddenly be closed out simply because they have a socialist form of government. So what we could do is try to deepen our influence around the world by working with people instead of making it an ideological problem and suggesting that there's a domino theory where once one government becomes socialist or communist or pinko or whatever you might call it, it is bound to have more influence on its neighbors than we can. That's never been proved.

"Wouldn't it be much wiser and more far-seeing if we decided that the way we could be most influential with socialist governments is to try to work with them and help them and trade with them because they're willing to trade with us. So it is not they who close the door. It is we who close the door. They do need trade as well. They need it of course on an equitable basis."—Tom Gervasi

* * *

Both trade and aid are inextricably linked with perceived geo-political priorities. Since the signing of the Nkomati Accord, western food aid is flowing to Mozambique, but in December of 1984 as a result of the cynicism of super-power politics, there were just 137 tons of maize in this warehouse in Gaza province to last 600,000 people a month.

"It is morally wrong for a government to cut off flows of food or tents or clothing, whatever is needed to an acute emergency situation....Of course the British government has been moving further away from the humanitarian position, or at least the appearance of one, further towards the U.S. position that aid is strictly strategic and strictly to do with British interests...especially now that the development aid system is being taken over by the Foreign Office very directly and the Minister responsible is a Foreign Office Minister, there's very little pretence that independent judgments about development or aid are being made. It's all now political and to do with Foreign Office objectives. So whichever government is doing things that the British government likes to see, if they vote the right way in the U.N. for instance, or on a much bigger scale, if they're pursuing policies in their particular region that the British want to encourage, that all adds up to a big aid program. I'm not saying that the Soviet Bloc is any better, not at all. But it is the Western governments which claim moral superiority or an attachment to democracy; if they can't produce something that actually matches these fine phrases, then they really should be called into question. In many ways the Soviet Union and its satellites are less useful to a developing country because they are much less experienced and they don't really learn the sophistication of aid methods which the Westerners have done. If you go to any School of Development Studies, you'll find that it has become so sophisticated as to be incomprehensible. The whole thing is being quantified, it's all about cost benefit analysis and if you stood up in a seminar at one of these Schools of Development, in fact, and tried to talk about some basic humanitarian ideas, you'd be laughed out of court. But in the Soviet system they don't have this kind of sophistication and so it's a matter of rather what we would see as outdated ideas. I mean the extreme example, which did happen in the '60s, was snow ploughs to middle of Central Africa, for instance. I mean it's really happened. And although it's not quite as obvious, the same sort of ghastly mistakes keep being made. And at the same time, of course, the Soviet Bloc don't tend to just hand out aid or give loans; they tend to do various kind's of commodity barter deals. There are very heavy strings attached, where you have to take the Soviet advisers to go with the equipment....And a lot of countries have reacted very strongly against the Soviet approach to aid giving. But it's heavily tied, politically, in a more obvious way even than Western aid."—BARBARA ROGERS

Russian armaments land at Maputo port alongside Western grain; both necessary for the county's survival, as both donor blocs pressure Mozambique for its allegiance. But it may be too late. Because of the years without help and the continued backing of the M.N.R., by October 1986 the forecast was that three million people were suffering the effects of primary malnutrition and without massive grain supplies, fuel and transport they would all die.[7] But the war goes on and as the U.S. Senate voted to overturn President Reagan's veto on their sanctions against South Africa, Mr. Pic Botha, the South African Foreign Minister, threatened in a television interview that the sanctions would cause him to effectively cut off food supplies to the Front-Lines States.

It is by no means clear who will win this square on the geo-political chess board, the West or the Soviet Union, neither is it clear who will win internally, FRELIMO or the M.N.R. But what is quite clear is that with continuing war and drought and economic manipulation by external powers, Mozambicans and their independence will be the losers.

"American foreign policy's always difficult to figure out and I think it's particularly difficult in this administration. It seems clear to me that our practice or our policy in Mozambique really is to undermine the Soviet position, and I think the reason is that it seems fairly clear that the Soviets are giving a lower priority to southern Africa now. They've got great economic problems at home; they've got problems in eastern Europe and so forth, and they're not prepared to put the kind of money into Mozambique and pehaps into other countries in Third World areas that they once were. They haven't had the success in the Third World that I think many people thought they might have a decade ago, and so I think the American policy clearly is to get into Mozambique in every way they legally can, in the hope of winning that regime away from the Soviet Union. We don't do that in many other cases. There are other cases—Central America, for example—in which we take exactly the opposite position, but consistency has never been one of our strong points."—DICK CLARKE, Aspen Institute for Humanitarian Studies

"George Hauser has said that Henry Kissinger's attitude towards policy in Africa was that it reflected a global strategy in which African realities were secondary to a perceived Soviet challenge, and I think that's probably accurate. It's not to say that American policy does not interest itself in the well-being of Third World populations for their own sake, but that really becomes secondary. In many places around the globe we don't get involved even though the conditions and situations may be just as critical or devastating as they are in places where we do get involved.... So often the only criteria for where we do get involved is that it has played some role in the East/West struggle."—CONGRESSMAN TED WEISS

"I don't think we have any strategic aspirations vis-à-vis Mozambique. We would like to see a non-aligned Mozambique and have a full and productive relationship there that would include active assistance programs, in the first instance, in the famine emergency, but more importantly in the field of economic development."—CHESTER CROCKER

"Well I'm sure that America's interest in Mozambique is anti-Soviet. I mean we've never shown any interest in any country in Africa that I know of for any other reason, certainly in southern Africa—so I'm sure it's strategic."
—DICK CLARKE

"Beginning from Angola in 1975, when the M.P.L.A., the Angola government, was faced with a South African invasion and the C.I.A. inspired invasion from Zaire, the feeling in South Africa and the Western allies was that there was literally a revolutionary wave sweeping down southern Africa which might overwhelm politically, ideologically that subcontinent, and they decided to stem the tide of this wave."—BEREKET SELASSIE

"We did believe we had to reassert Western leadership and American leadership in a region where we had been on the receiving end for six of seven years in a row. There was a negative trend for sure. We were determined to reverse that trend. *We do not accept any legitimate right of foreign intervention by our global adversary in southern Africa.*"—DR. CHESTER CROCKER. (Emphasis added.)

Whatever Washington and Moscow and latterly Peking may want to believe, the world does not belong to them. There are over two hundred other nations on this planet and to my knowledge they have never individually or collectively agreed that the super powers could use it as their battleground. Global adversaries indeed! That may seem an over-simplistic and obvious statement but it is none the less true. However, for as long as they continue to regard each other as global adversaries, they will do nothing but add to the turmoil and carnage that is the legacy of imperial domination and interference.

"I think there has been a view that the United States and the Western democracies generally should remain prepared to fight wars throughout this entire period, and that communism was a successor to fascism as a threat to the kind of moderate liberal order—economically and politically—that the United States felt was important to protect and expand in the world. And the whole dynamic I think of decolonization created a very big theater in which this policy was played out, supposedly as part of protecting Western interests, but I think largely as a matter of extending the reach of Western capital and Western power, and particularly U.S. power and capital."—PROFESSOR RICHARD FALK

THAI/ KAMPUCHEA BORDER

"...to the last Cambodian"

Straddled along the ill-defined border between Kampuchea and Thailand are a number of what the United Nations calls "border encampments." Despite the presence of thousands of women and children, these are not refugee camps, but military bases. They are controlled by Pol Pot's Khmer Rouge army and their partners in the so-called Kampuchean coalition whose other forces are the right-wing K.P.N.L.F. army of Son San, a former prime minister under Prince Sihanouk, and a few of his followers.

When the Khmer Rouge fled to Thailand, at the time of the Vietnamese liberation of Kampuchea, they took thousands of peasants with them. As famine and disease held Kampuchea in their grip during 1979 and '80, tens of thousands more crossed the border, lured by the plentiful supplies of rice and other relief goods that were being distributed tons at a time with few restrictions, while the international agencies demanded impossible conditions before delivering supplies to Phnom Penh. And then the circus of aid agencies and the press moved in and "The Border" was for a while big news. Rosalind Carter came to see for herself and press men trod on skeletal children to get the best shot of the First Lady. People the world over who had reacted with such compassion and generosity to "Year Zero," the documentary film about the genocide and famine in Kampuchea that journalist John Pilger and I made in 1979, once more opened their hearts and their checkbooks to help; and most people working in the border area kept quiet about the fact that much of the aid there was being delivered directly to the Khmer Rouge. In 1980 one official blurted out, off the record, "All we're doing is feeding an army!"[1]

By the Fall of 1980 that army, which most politicians admit are the most thorough mass-murderers since Hitler and the Nazis, had been resuscitatated with food and emergency services provided by supposedly caring governments whose people were kept in the dark about this other dimension to the story.

Aid can and does save lives, and fortunately people did begin to recover and kids were no longer lying around like piles of matchwood. So the story died, and the press moved on. But the fighters also recovered and continued their attacks against Kampuchean civilians. The Thai government continued to permit Peking to deliver shipments of arms and ammunition to the fighters and at the same time gave free rein to the Kampuchean Emergency Group, otherwise known as K.E.G., to "oversee" the border. K.E.G. was a specially created unit of the U.S. State Department and worked through their embassy in Bangkok. Officially its function was to provide a group of experts who knew the "nitty gritty of aid" and who were "concerned that we have information on life-threatening situations that they [the refugees] may face."[2] But K.E.G. officers were not people who "knew the nitty gritty of aid," they were experts on the nitty gritty of clandestined war and destabilization. Michael Eiland, K.E.G.'s director, had been a major in the U.S. Special Forces in Vietnam and had been involved in Operation Daniel Boone, a series of secret and illegal ventures into Kampuchea that climaxed with Nixon's secret bombing.[3] Their non-publicized role was to ensure that the Khmer Rouge received the supplies they required so that the destabilization of Kampuchea and its government would be effective. Aid officials representing the international agencies talked at the time of "K.E.G. applying constant pressure to keep supplying the Khmer Rouge."[4]

However, this open manipulation of the international agencies became an embarrassment to both the agencies and the politicians, and in 1983 the United Nations Border Relief Operation (UNBRO) was created to take over the feeding. UNBRO cleverly adopted a new distribution system which officially gave "2.4 rations to every female over the age of ten"; what happened to the food after that was not their concern. Thus they were and are able to wash their hands of the responsibility of feeding the soldiers.

The object of the operation has echoes all over the globe and is governed by the perceived global adversarial relationship of the super powers and only indirectly concerns itself with Phnom Penh or Hanoi. Of course, there are those diehard types who can never forgive Vietnam for winning its independence or indeed accept that the U.S. completely screwed up in Kampuchea and "are trying to re-fight the Vietnam war and get a better result."[5] But those are only secondary issues.

The prime motivation for continuing support for the Khmer Rouge is to exert as much pressure as possible on the Soviet Union who at present is backing Hanoi and Phnom Penh to the tune of approximately $5 million per day. For the time being at least, this yearly drain of almost $2 billion on the Soviet economy is calculated to hurt Moscow more than normalized relations and trade with Vietnam would benefit the U.S.—balance sheets all over again. This is not simply conjecture; facts, figures and U.S. Government statements leave one in no doubt.

There are approximately five million people living in Kampuchea and about two hundred and forty thousand living in the border encampments. In 1983/4, total western governmental aid to the country was a pitiful $6 million, but for the same period aid to the Khmer Rouge and the civilians on the border was $39 million. That works out at $1.20 for each Kampuchean in the country but $162.50 for those on the border. Clearly the West prefers to take care of killers rather than their victims. Of course, the argument which says we can't stop the feeding because the civilians would suffer, is the same argument that says sanctions cannot be applied to South Africa without hurting the Black population. Of course it would hurt them, but they are already hurting, every day, and every day the non-application of sanctions or the continued feeding on the border further enslaves them.

The propaganda machine that educates the mainly peasant population of the border encampments, be they civilian or fighters, is extremely effective. People are taught on the one hand to fear the Phnom Penh government and its allies the Vietnamese, and on the other to believe that their salvation lies in the hands of America and its allies, the Khmer Rouge and China. Aid workers and evangelists filter through the camps distributing local rice and American dreams, tranquillizers and T-shirts, seemingly oblivious to the fact that these two hundred thousand Kampucheans are still being held as a human shield by the Khmer Rouge whose raids deep into Kampuchea and increasingly against Thai villages show no sign of letting up. Futhermore, it should not be forgotten that all that stands between the Kampuchean people and the return of the Khmer Rouge is the Vietnamese army, which would like to go home but obviously cannot, but whose withdrawal is demanded by the U.S. and the ASEAN countries along with their European allies.

> "The U.S. will fight the Vietnamese to the last Cambodian."—Journalist, Bangkok

And if there was still any doubt in your mind, the U.S. goverment has given over $85 million directly to the Khmer Rouge since 1980 in the form of development assistance and military aid.[6]

> "We will seek, if we can, to find ways to increase the political, economic and, yes, military pressure on Vietnam."—JOHN HOLDRIDGE, U.S. Assistant Secretary of State for East Asia[7]

What is worth noting is that Secretary Holdridge made this remark during an address he gave at the American Club in Peking.

> "Those countries that are giving the aid give it for these particular displaced persons, particular refugees, although they're not called refugees, but...those people who are in the area for reasons of their own, political reasons of their own. They want to assist these people; they don't want to give assistance to Kampuchea and its government, which they don't recognize, but that is a political problem to be discussed in the capitals of the member states and the capitals of donor countries, not with the UN. It would be naïve to think that you can have, so close to the border of a country where there's so much political turmoil, a non-political situation. But this being said, the United Nations does and must do its best to distribute the assistance purely on a humanitarian basis. Now...once that humanitarian assistance is given to those people in the border area that they in turn should use it in some way...there is very little, very little we can do. I don't think anybody would deny that, that there are problems. What the U.N. does and tries to do is to minimize them and be very careful about the way things are being run, but there's a point that comes when the U.N. cannot do any more. It is not on it's sovereign territory, it is not running these areas...."
>
> *"But it is running that border relief operation. It has blanket organizational control of the whole of that border area."*

"Yes, but when you say the U.N. is feeding combatants and is, is encouraging fighters..."

"I did not say they were encouraging fighters."

"All right, feeding them in order that they can go to combat. There comes a time when you cannot really any more say, well, this child is not going to become a combatant. I mean how can we know it?"

"But there is a distinction between a six-or-seven-year-old child and a twenty- or twenty-five-year-old adult male carrying a Kalashnikof or an M16. The border—you've been there—the border is crawling with them. Ampil for example, which was recently over-run, it was a military camp."

"But if I may say so, Ampil is in Kampuchean territory and it is not run by the U.N."

"The camp may not be run by the U.N. but the camp is supplied by the U.N. and U.N. have facilities there, they have their own tents there with U.N. on the roofs."

"What happens is that some of the men in the camp will go out of the camps and go into Thailand and then rejoin their families and maybe indeed they have the use of the U.N. supplies, but I mean how can you stop that?"

"The U.N. is being manipulated. Its offices on the border are being used. Its expertise is being used....."

"The U.N. is, well I mean inasmuch as the U.N. is helping people survive, that out of this group of people may come fighters and combatants. In that sense, yes, of course, but this is not either the purpose or the idea.... We do our best but we, you know, if something goes wrong beyond what we can do, then it is no longer our responsibility."—FRANCOIS GIULIANI, U.N. Spokesman

"There is an increasing feeling that we would support anti-government guerrilla groups—certainly this administration wants to do that in Nicaragua and certainly in Indo-China. Whatever comes along has to be geared and centered on this core problem of how we defeat the Soviet Union in this struggle."—DICK CLARKE

Conclusion

Nowhere is this dominance and exploitation of the Third World by the First more clearly seen than in Southeast Asia. The constant political, economic and military pressure has left the Indo-Chinese countries trapped in the nineteenth century making them now some of the poorest in the world.[1] Western economic isolation is driving them into a deeper and more subservient relationship with the Soviet Union, a relationship that neither Kampuchea nor Vietnam wants—the Vietnamese would hardly have fought for thirty years for what they have now. Surely no one can imagine that. "I lived through the French period, then the American period and now the Russian period. This is not what we fought for, this is not what Ho meant when he talked of independence."

The ironies in all this would be laughable were they not so tragic, Why did the United States fight for so long to deny the Vietnamese their independence? To halt the spread of advancing communism from China; or so we were told by successive presidents. In reality it was an attempt to retain regional strategic and therefore economic control, particularly through the use of the bases at Da Nang and Cam Ranh Bay. "He who controls that coastline controls the South China Sea and the Gulf of Thailand, thereby ensuring shipping access to the East Asian markets which might be lost to China or worse still the Soviet Union" was how the reasoning went.

But who is the West's latest trading and strategic ally? China.

And who holds the all-important military bases today? The Soviet Union.

Has the Soviet Union really gained? Well, she hasn't taken the East Asian markets and it is costing the Soviet people $5 million a day. I suppose the Kremlin must feel that the Soviet people consider almost two billion dollars a year a small price to pay for an embryonic colony, though I bet they haven't asked them. Their presence in Vietnam has but one benefit in that they do get to antagonize both the U.S.A. and China.

Has the U.S. gained? Fifty-eight thousand dead Americans and their families wouldn't think so. Have they lost the East Asian market? No, and the Administration believes that even though they lost the battle they can still win the war. "If we can't have Vietnam, then we'll make damn sure that nobody else can, not even the Vietnamese" is what you feel is said behind the closed doors of the State Department. Having forced the Vietnamese into the waiting arms of the Soviet Union they are able to say, "You see, we told you so, once the South fell it would become just another Soviet satellite." In other words, it is useful as an example to discourage others. Propaganda, nothing more. The loss is turned into a gain. It intends to show that any radical nationalist movement that has the audacity to try to do things their way and seeks independence and a socialist system will find itself being forced into the penury of the Soviet camp.

And Peking? Well, they condemn a lot of their own people to death every time they try to invade Vietnam. But they do get to hurt the Vietnamese, to cause problems for the Soviet Union and an unending supply of Coca-Cola.

All that the people of Indochina get is war. All they ever wanted and still want is to be left alone. Had the geo-political chess game not been played with such cynicism on their land, at least five million Kampucheans, Laotians and Vietnamese would be alive today and peace and economic stability would prevail rather than the current turmoil.

But it doesn't end here. Afghanistan, Angola, Chad, Chile, Guatemala, Haiti, Iran, Iraq, Kurdistan, The Philippines, Poland, Western Sahara, Sri Lanka, Sudan, East Timor, Ulster, South Yemen.... You cannot call this peace.

In Britain, the home of the welfare state, schools are overcrowded because there isn't enough money to employ enough teachers on a living wage. Hospitals are overcrowded and understaffed too, again through lack of funds. Old people die alone regularly from hypothermia, because they cannot afford to heat themselves and the system cannot afford to look after them. Nearly four million people are unemployed and possibly as many as 18 million, or 30 percent of the population are now living on or below the poverty line[2] and still Whitehall insist that fully fifty per cent of our research and development funds should go on weapons.

Though the U.S. figures may be different, the end result for the American people is the same. Too many ordinary Americans are being ground into poverty as Washington spends more on weapons than at any time in history.

In the Soviet Union they still have a problem meeting minimum consumer

276

demands and have to import basic grains from the West in order to feed themselves, while Moscow affirms that she will match any challenge, will not be beaten economically, and the Soviet military takes the lion's share of the country's finances.

In the developing countries, at least 17,000,000 people die every year from hunger and hunger-related disease; 15,000,000 of them are children under five.[3] No one knows how many die because of the wars, but probably a quarter of a million were killed in the time it took me to make this journey. If total spending on weapons was simply halved it would provide $27,000 for each one of those 17,000,000. But it would only cost a fraction of that to save their lives and provide funds so that those people could develop their countries and prosper and no longer need the support of the developed world. In other words, we'd all be better off.

Despite the massive spending on so-called defense, the world is less secure now than at any time in its history. We squander more and more money on weapons but succeed only in raising tensions. Meanwhile we condemn millions of people in the developing world to lives of misery, hopelessness and early death.

> "We are involved in a resource war. We are basically taking things out and putting nothing back. It's a one-way street. Many Third World countries begin to realize this and try to go independent... and that's when we send in the Marines, which we've done on innumerable occasions in just this century."—TOM GERVASI

> "Of the eighteen times on the public record that the United States has threatened to use nuclear weapons, sixteen of them have been in conventional conflicts or interventions. We must understand that the seeds of nuclear war lie in interventions or conventional conflicts."—DR. CHARLIE CLEMMENTS

> "If you look carefully you'll see that these fundamental issues—should we rely on nuclear weapons, should we intervene in the Third World—have never been discussed, much less have the American people been given an alternative."—PROFESSOR RICHARD FALK

If one suggests change we are told, "We cannot cut back on our military spending, it is vital for our national defense." But most of the weapons and systems purchased are offensive, not defensive.

If you ask where the justification lies in selling arms to the Third World whereby wars are fueled, "Supply and demand, old boy."

If you mention that in current nuclear arsenals there is the explosive power of two tons of TNT for every human being on this planet and therefore surely we could stop, or at least cut back, they say, "Just won't work and it would be death economically." No it wouldn't, not according to the Congressional Budget Office and Chase Econometrics. The problem is that the alternative has never been tried, not under today's conditions or any other. Not since the first arms salesman and inventor of dynamite, Alfred Nobel, he of the peace price no less, has the arms industry done anything other than grow.

Every day billions are syphoned off into weapons research, development and manufacture, and in so doing civilian industry is not only denied capital, it is denied something even more priceless—access to the benefit of clearly brilliant minds. What kind of world might we live in if all those inventive and imaginative people were employed in researching and developing industries and innovations that enhance life rather than destroy it.

This book has been as much about the unlearned lessons of our history as it has been about the cynicism of geo-politics and the misery, barbarity and futility of war in the Third world today. But history is not something that happens in spite of us. It is not an external force over which we have no control. We are living it. In it, through it—and therefore contribute to its making. We do not need the benefit of hindsight to see that the policies haven't really changed and don't work any better today than they did forty years ago. All of the information in this book was easy to obtain and though, admittedly, many of the government documents were not freely available to the public twenty or forty years ago, they were distributed to the policy makers, and the press certainly knew. Whether it was the turning of Ho Chi Minh from an ally to an enemy— "Were it not for our 'communist blinders,' Ho could well have served the larger purpose of America"—or the Soviet cessation of support for Eritrea, and the subsequent backing of the Derg while thousands starved, the facts have been known, the decisions taken in spite of the facts.

I find it completely incomprehensible that the people of the developed world, at least in the West, who continually boast that they live within democracies, do not exercise their democratic rights, if nothing else, for their own benefit let alone the benefit to the Third World. If this madness is to be changed it can only come by practicing democracy, not talking about it. Democracy should mean control of government by the people, not control of the people by government. In truth most people in the West simply practice a masquerade of democracy for just a few seconds once every four or five years by putting crosses on ballot papers. Thereafter, they exercise no control over government at all. However, the system of parliamentary representation does exist, it just has to be used. By our apathy and silence we perpetuate this madness to the detriment of everyone.

The proponents of this insanity would probably criticize all of these arguments by saying that they are too idealistic. Is it wrong to hold ideals for a better quality of life for all? They would also comment that these arguments are too simple, that they don't take into account the complications of the modern world. But it is they who make the world complicated and they who

278

confuse the argument. In the end it is very simple. Do we want to continue to stand by and watch the people of the developing world have their lives torn apart? Do we want to continue to subsidize this killing? Do we want to wait on the sideline as one or more of these wars inextricably sucks in the super powers and leads to the use of nuclear weapons? Do we want to live or don't we?

The nations of the developing world don't want to fight us; most of them don't want to fight each other either; they simply want to be left in peace, and free. We make them fight through our greed, intransigence and archaic militarism.

When a peasant in El Salvador picks up a rifle and fires at a multi-million-dollar jet, frankly that peasant has more in common with a peasant of Afghanistan or Eritrea than either one of the ideologies of the super powers they're struggling against. To them Western imperialism or Soviet imperialism appears much the same—it is supporting those who would thwart their aspirations for a better life.

The world does not *have* to fight wars. It is not a necessary function of our species. There are alternative ways of reaching solutions to problems, but the current system in many cases precludes them. Politicians and generals may start wars, but people have to fight them. People who don't talk like us or look like us or share exactly the same political views are not the enemy. Not the Russians or the Mozambicans, not the Palestinians or the Eritreans, not the Vietnamese or the Nicaraguans, none of them is the enemy. War is the enemy.

Source Notes

N.B. The decisions regarding noting sources herein have been arbitrary and reflect interest rather than revelation. I have not bothered in the following notes to include all sources, since much of the information is widely available and can be found within the titles listed in the Recommended Bibliography. To the best of my ability and knowledge, all facts within this book are correct.

Part One

1. I.T.N. recording of Margaret Thatcher during 1983 election.
2. P.P.S./23. Feb. 24, 1948. Excerpted in *Containment*, edited by Thomas H. Etzold and John Lewis Gaddis (New York: Columbia University Press, 1978), pp. 226/7.

Source Notes

NICARAGUA

1. *International Herald Tribune*/Washington Post Service. Dec. 8, 1982.
2. Ibid.
3. Tom Barry and Deb Preusch, *The Central America Fact Book* (New York; Grove Press, 1986), p. 230.
4. Carleton Beals, *With Sandino in Nicaragua,* p. 341.
5. *Guardian* (London).
6. Nicaragua v. U.S.A.. Judgment of the International Court of Justice. The Hague, Netherlands, June 27, 1986, paras. 93 and 94.
7. Ibid., p. 43.
8. Ibid.
9. Arms Control and Foreign Policy Caucus of U.S. Senate: *Who Are the Contras?*
10. *London Times,* Nov. 7, 1984, quoting observers from Washington Office on Latin America and International Human Rights Law Group.
11. Report of the National Bipartisan Commission on Central America, Jan 10, 1984, pp. 93.
12. Press statement, Feb. 17,1981.
13. Taken from interview with Tom Gervasi by author.

LEBANON

1. David McDowall, *Lebanon: A conflict of minorities.* Minority Rights Group (U.K.). Report No: 61, 1983, p. 3.
2. Ibid.
3. Alexander M. Haig, Jr., *Caveat* (London: Wiedenfeld and Nicholson, 1984), p. 329.
4. Jonathan Randal, *The Tragedy of Lebanon* (London: Chatto and Windus, 1983), p. 244.
5. Haig, op. cit. p. 337.
6. Randal, op. cit. p. 249.
7. Ibid. p. 257.
8. Ibid. p. 254 and interview by author with Dr. Amal Shama'a, Barbir Hospital.
9. Michael Jansen, *The Battle of Beirut* (Zed Press, 1982), p. 30, and interviews by author.
10. McDowall, op. cit. p. 3.
11. Jansen, op. cit. p. 29.
12. The Commission of Inquiry into events at the Refugee Camps in Beirut: Final Report. Feb. 8, 1983, p. 63.
13. Statistics resultant from surveys conducted on behalf of the Zahara Hospital, Beirut, 1984. Also interview by author of Dr. Mansour.

ERITREA

1. David Pool, *Eritrea: Africa's Longest War.* Anti Slavery Society for the Protection of Human Rights. Report No:3, 1982, p. 42.

VIETNAM/KAMPUCHEA

1. Archimedes L.A. Patti, *Why Viet Nam?* (University of California Press, 1980), p. 392.
2. Ibid.
3. Michael Maclear, *Vietnam: The Ten Thousand Day War* (London Thames Methuen, 1981), p. 22.
4. Patti, op. cit. p. 52.
5. DOS MEMO 2 Feb. 1950. National Archives. Dean Acheson to President Truman. (Also Patti, op. cit. p. 389.)
6. Patti, op. cit. p. 391.
7. Ibid. p. 129.
8. Edgar Snow, *The Other Side of the River—Red China Today,* p. 686. (Also Patti, op. cit. p. 325.)
9. Patti, op. cit. p. 250. Translated by Patti's staff.
10. Congressional Research Service Library of Congress. *THE U.S. GOVERNMENT AND THE VIETNAM WAR—Executive and Legislative Roles and Relationships. Part 1. 1945-1961,* April 1984 (S.Prt. 98-185 Pt1), p. 64.
11. Ibid. Foreword, p.v.
12. Ronald Reagan. Election Campaign, 1980.
13. Michael Kidron and Dan Smith, *The War Atlas* (London: Pan Books Ltd., 1983), Graphic 38. (Also SIPRI Yearbook 1982.)
14. From interviews by author and statistics collated by Ministry of Health SRVN.
15. *Vietnam: A Television History.* Central Independent Television plc(UK)/ WGBH(Boston), 1983.
16. Maclear, op. cit. p. 405.
17. Jean Delvert, *La Paysannerie Khmere avant 1970* (Mondes en Developement No.28., 1979), p. 739. (Also Ben Kiernan *How Pol Pot Came to Power,* Verso, 1980, p.xiv.)
18. Kiernan, op. cit. p. 350.
19. Research by author and John Pilger in Kampuchea, Aug. 1979, included in their documentary film: *Year Zero—The Silent Death of Cambodia,* ATV Network Ltd. (UK), 1979.
20. Guenter Lewy. *America in Vietnam* (Oxford University Press, 1978), p. 257.
21. Robert Harris and Jeremy Paxman, *A Higher Form of Killing* (London: Triad/Granada—Paladin, 1983), pp. 191-92.

22. SIPRI 1982, op. cit., also Kidron and Smith, Map 38.
23. John Pilger, *Heroes* (London: Jonathan Cape, 1986). p. 275. Also confirmed by State Department.

EL SALVADOR

1. Robert Armstrong and Janet Shenk, *El Salvador, the Face of Revolution* (Pluto Press (UK), 1982), p. 27.
2. James Dunkerley, *The Long War* (Junction Books (UK), 1982), p. 25.
3. Tom Barry and Deb Preusch, *The Central America Fact Book* (New York: Grove Press, Inc., 1986), p. 200.
4. Ibid.
5. Armstrong and Shenk, op. cit. p. 77.
6. Dunkerley, op. cit. p. 76.
7. Barry and Preusch, op. cit. p. 200.
8. *New York Times*, Oct. 11, 1983.
9. Dunkerley, op. cit., p. 203.
10. Americas Watch, August 1986.
11. Dermot Keogh, *Romero—El Salvador's Martyr* (Dublin: Dominican Publications, 1981), p. 99.
12. Report to the Arms Control and Foreign Policy Caucus of the House of Representatives, Feb. 1985.
13. Ibid.
14. Edward L. King. Testimony before the Sub-Committee on Western Hemisphere Affairs of the House Committee on Foreign Affairs, 1985.
15. Barry and Preusch, op. cit., p. 212.

PART TWO

1. Many euphemisms collected over the years by author. Some appear in Jonathan Green's *Newspack—Dictionary of Jargon* (London: Routledge and Kegan Paul, 1984).
2. Author's calculation based on interviews with exhibitors at Farnborough '84. Average: $420,000 per exhibitor, 600 exhibitors.
3. Tom Gervasi, *The Arsenal of Democracy III: America's War Machine* (New York: Grove Press, 1984), p. 4.
4. Campaign Against the Arms Trade (CAAT).
5. a/a.
6. a/a.
7. Gervasi, op. cit., p. 3.
8. CAAT.
9. U.S. Arms Control and Disarmament Agency (ACDA) and World Health Organization (WHO).
10. ITN Report, Sept. 1986.

E<small>RITREA</small> 2

1. Ceasefire offer contained in ITN Channel 4 extended report by author, broadcast Feb. 1985.

M<small>OZAMBIQUE</small>

1. Jospeh Hanlon, *Mozambique: The Revolution Under Fire* (Zed Books Ltd (UK), 1984), p. 255.
2. Ibid.
3. Ibid. p. 234.
4. FRELIMO.
5. Hanlon, op. cit. p. 235.
6. Ibid. p. 234.

N<small>ICARAGUA</small> 2

N1. Nicaragua v. U.S.A., op. cit., Note 6, p. 39, para 86.
N2. Document leaked to author by Labour member of House of Commons.

M<small>OZAMBIQUE</small> 2

7. ITN report, Oct. 1986.

T<small>HAI</small>/K<small>AMPUCHEAN</small> Border

1. Documentary film *Year One,* by John Pilger and author. A.T.V. Network Ltd., 1980.
2. Ibid. Interview with Lionel Rosenblatt, spokesperson for K.E.G.
3. William Shawcross, *Sideshow* (London: Andre Deutsch, 1979), p. 25.
4. *Year One,* op. cit.
5. Ibid. Interview with Paul Quinn Judge, American Friends Field Service.
6. Congressional Research Service.
7. *International Herald Tribune,* from *Washington Post,* Oct. 1981.

C<small>ONCLUSION</small>

1. World bank.
2. Pilger, op. cit., p. 503.
3. UNICEF

Glossary

N.B. The following glossary of names, terms and acronyms is only of those mentioned in the text, many others exist in the countries and areas covered. For further information refer to recommended bibliography.

Nicaragua

F.S.L.N.	*Frente Sandinista de Liberacion Nacional.* Sandinista National Liberation Front.
Sandinista/Sandinist	Originally supporter of Augosto Sandino, now supporter of F.S.L.N.
Sandinismo	The ideology of Sandino and F.S.L.N.
Contras	*Contra Revolutionarios.* Counter Revolutionaries.
F.D.N.	*Fuerza Democratica Nicaraguense.* Nicaraguan Democratic Force. Political organization of the Contras.
ARDE	*Alianza Revolutionario Democratica.* Revolutionary Democratic Alliance. Counter Revolutionary Army of former Sandinista Eden Pastora. (Disbanded June 1986.)
O.A.S.	Organization of American States.

Lebanon

P.L.O.	Palestine Liberation Organization.
P.L.A.	Palestine Liberation Army.
AMAL	Shi'ite Political Party and Militia.
P.S.P.	Druze's Progressive Socialist Party and Militia of the Jumblatt Family.
Kata'ib	Also known as Phalange. Maronite Christian Militia of the Gemayel family.
Ahrar	National Liberal party and Militia of Chamoun Family. Violently taken over by Gemayel family (1978) and amalgamated with Kata'ib to form the Lebanese Forces.
I.D.F.	Israeli Defense Forces.
I.P.F.	International Peace Keeping Force. (France, Italy, U.S. troops deployed in Lebanon August 1982)

Eritrea

E.P.L.F.	Eritrean Peoples Liberation Front.
E.P.L.A.	Eritrean Peoples Liberation Army.
E.R.A.	Eritrean Relief Association.
Derg	Ruling committee of Ethiopia.
O.A.U.	Organization of African Unity.

Vietnam

V.N./S.R.V.	Democratic VietNam (1945)/ Democratic Republic of Vietnam (1975).
N.V.A.	Peoples Army of North Vietnam.
N.L.F.	National Liberation Front.
P.L.A.F.	Peoples Liberation Armed Forces (of N.L.F.).
V.C.	Viet Cong. Pejorative American name for P.L.A.F.
VIETMINH	Vietnamese League for Independence. *Viet Nam Doc Lap Dong Minh Hoi.*
A.R.V.N.	Army of the Republic of (South) Vietnam
COSVN	Central Office of South Vietnam. American Army name for P.L.A.F./N.V.A. command H.Q.
ASEAN	Association of South East Asian Nations.

Kampuchea

Khmer	The race of people inhabiting Kampuchea.
Khmer Rouge	Red Khmers. Name given by Prince Noradom Sihanouk to Pol Pot and his followers of the Kampuchean Communist Party.
The Angkar	The Organization (on high). Name used by Khmer Rouge fighters when referring to the high command.

El Salvador

F.M.L.N.	*Frente Farabundo Marti para la Liberacion Nacional.* Farabundo Marti National Liberation Front. Military umbrella command of four guerrilla armies representing center to left wing groups.
Muchacho(s)	"The Boy(s)." Guerrilla fighter(s) of F.M.L.N.
F.D.R.	*Frente Democratico Revolutionario.* Democratic Revolutionary Front. Umbrella organization for political parties of center and left representing the F.M.L.M.
P.C.N.	*Partido de Conciliation Nacional.* National Party of Conciliation. Military's political party.
P.D.C.	*Partido Democrata Cristiano.* Christian Democrats.
ARENA	*Alianza Republicana Nacionalista.* National Republican Alliance. Extreme right-wing party of Roberto D'Aubuisson.

Glossary

ORDEN	*Organizacion Democratica Nacionalista.* National Democratic Organization. Part-time civil/military terror squads.
MAP	U.S. Military Assistance Program.
ESF	U.S. Economic Support Fund
IMET	U.S. International Military Education and Training Program.
FMS	Foreign Military Sales.

Mozambique

FRELIMO	*Frente de Libertacao de Mozambique.* Front for the Liberation of Mozambique. Won Liberation for Mozambique from Portugal (1975).
M.N.R.	*Resistencia Nacional Mozambicana.* Mozambican National Resistance. Also known as RENAMO. Anti-Frelimo force created by Rhodesia and taken over by South Africa.
G.E.P.	*Grupo Especial Paraquedistas.* Portuguese Special Paratroop Group. (Anti-Frelimo force during independence war. Members became M.N.R.)
PIDE	*Policia Internacional e de Defensa do Estado.* Portuguese secret police in Mozambique (became DGS in 1969).
Front-Line States.	Angola, Botswana, Mozambique, Tanzania, Zambia, Zimbabwe.
A.N.C.	African National Congress. Political and armed resistance to South African government.
M.P.L.A.	Peoples Movement for the Liberation of Angola, now the government.

Organizations

I.C.R.C.	International Committee of the Red Cross.
UNBRO	United Nations Border Relief Operation (Thailand/ Kampuchea border).
UNDP	United Nations Development Program.
UNFAO	United Nations Food and Agricultural Organization.
UNHCR	United Nations High Commission for Refugees.
UNICEF	United Nations Children Fund.
UNIFIL	United Nations Interim Force in Lebanon.
W.F.P.	World Food Program.
I.A.D.B.	Inter American Development Bank. Branch of World Bank.
COMECON.	Council of Mutual Economic Assistance (Russian)
U.S. AID	United States Agency for International Development.

Recommended Bibliography

Central America
Dollars & Dictators—A guide to Central America. Tom Barry, Beth Wood, Deb Preusch. The Resource Center (USA), Zed Press (UK), 1982.
The Central America Fact Book. Tom Barry and Deb Preusch. Grove Press, 1986.
Kissinger's Kingdom? Stuart Holland M.P. and Donald Anderson M.P. Spokesman. 1984.
In Contempt of Congress. Institute of Policy Studies, Washington DC., 1986.
Turning the Tide. Noam Chomsky. South End Press, 1985.
Under the Big Stick. Karl Bermann. South End Press, 1986.
Witness to War. Charles Clemments. Bantam Books, 1984.
Under the Eagle. Jenny Pearce. Latin American Bureau (UK), 1982.
El Salvador—Central America in the New Cold War. Marvin E. Gettleman and others. Grove Press, 1982.
El Salvador—The Face of Revolution. Robert Armstrong and Janet Shenk. Pluto Press (UK), South End Press (USA), 1982.
The Long War—Dictatorship and Revolution in El Salvador. James Dunkerley. Junction Books (UK), 1982.
Romero—El Salvador's Martyr. Dermot Keogh. Dominican Publications, Dublin, Ireland, 1981.
Somoza. Bernard Diederich. Junction Books (UK), 1982.
Bitter Fruit—The Untold Story of the American Coup in Guatemala. Stephen Schlesinger and Stephen Kinzer. Sinclair Browne (UK).

Middle East
The Battle of Beirut: Why Israel Invaded Lebanon. Michael Jansen. Zed Press (UK), 1982.
Surviving the Siege of Beirut. Linda Mikdadi. Onyx Press, 1983.
The Fateful Triangle. Noam Chomsky. Pluto Press (UK), South End Press (USA), 1983.
The Tragedy of Lebanon. Jonathan Randal. Chatto and Windus. (UK), 1983.
The PLO and Palestine. Abdallah Frangi. Zed Books (UK), 1982.
The Palestinian Liberation Organization. Helena Cobban. Cambridge University Press, 1984.

The Beirut Massacre (The Complete Kahan Commission Report). Karz-Cohl (NYC), 1983.
Lebanon, A Conflict of Minorities. David McDowall. Minority Rights Group Ltd, 1983.

Eritrea
Eritrea, Africa's longest war. David Pool. Anti-Slavery Society, 1979.
Behind the War in Eritrea. Basil Davidson and others. Spokesman, 1980.

Vietnam/Kampuchea
America in Vietnam. Guenter Lewy. Oxford University Press, 1978.
Vietnam Voices. Compiled by John Clark Pratt. Viking, Penguin Inc., 1984.
Vietnam—The Ten Thousand Day War. Michael MacLear. Thames Methuen, 1981.
Vietnam Reconsidered. Edited by Harrison E. Salisbury. Harper and Row, 1984.
Why Viet Nam. Archimedes L.A. Patti. University of California Press, 1980.
Heroes. John Pilger. Jonathan Cape Ltd., 1986.
The Last Day. Mirror Group Newspapers Ltd., 1975.
Catapult to Freedom. Wilfred Burchett. Quartet Books, 1978.
Sideshow. William Shawcross. Andre Deutsch, 1979.
How Pol Pot Came to Power. Ben Kiernan. Verso, 1985.
The China, Cambodia, Vietnam Triangle. Wilfred Burchett. Zed Press, 1981.

Mozambique
Mozambique: The Revolution Under Fire. Joseph Hanlon. Zed Books Ltd., 1984.

General
The War Atlas. Michael Kidron and Dan Smith. Pluto Press, 1983.
Herbicides in War. Edited by Arthur H. Westing. SIPRI (Sweden), 1984.
A Higher form of Killing. Robert Harris and Jeremy Paxman. Triad/Granada (UK), 1983.
Arsenal of Democracy III: Americas War Machine. Tom Gervasi. Grove Press, 1984.
The Myth of Soviet Military Supremacy, Tom Gervasi. Harper and Row, 1986.
Reagan's Secret Wars. Jay Peterzell. Center for National Security Studies, 1984.
Food, Poverty and Power. Anne Buchanan. Spokesman, 1982.
Of Bread and Guns. Nigel Harris. Penguin Books (UK), 1983.
How the Other Half Dies. Susan George. Penguin Books (UK), 1976.